Powers of Diaspora

Powers of Diaspora

TWO ESSAYS ON
THE RELEVANCE OF
JEWISH CULTURE

Jonathan Boyarin
and
Daniel Boyarin

University of Minnesota Press
Minneapolis / London

A different version of "Circumscribing Constitutional Identities in *Kiryas Joel*" appeared as a Note in *Yale Law Journal* 106, no. 5 (March 1997). Reprinted by permission of *Yale Law Journal*.

Published by the University of Minnesota Press
111 Third Avenue South, Suite 290
Minneapolis, MN 55401-2520
http://www.upress.umn.edu

Library of Congress Cataloging-in-Publication Data

Boyarin, Jonathan.
    Powers of diaspora : two essays on the relevance of Jewish culture / Jonathan Boyarin and Daniel Boyarin.
        p.   cm.
    ISBN 0-8166-3596-X (hc) — ISBN 0-8166-3597-8 (pbk.)
    1. Jewish diaspora—Political aspects.   2. Jewish diaspora—Political aspects—Case studies.   3. Masculinity—Religious aspects—Judaism.   4. Talmud—Criticism, interpretation, etc.   5. Kiryas Joel (N.Y.)—Ethnic relations—Political aspects.   6. Satmar Hasidim—Legal status, laws, etc.—New York (State)—Kiryas Joel.   I. Boyarin, Daniel.   II. Title.
    DS134 .B68 2002
    305.892'4—dc21

                                                            2001007374

12 11 10 09 08 07 06 05 04 03 02   10 9 8 7 6 5 4 3 2 1

Contents

To Elissa Sampson and to Chava Boyarin

Preface

Herein two brothers seek to evoke the diasporic genius of
Jewishness, that genius that consists in the exercise and preservation of cultural power separate from the coercive power
of the state. To say that such diasporic power exists *outside
of history* would surely risk confusion, for we are still not so
far from the days when Jewish absence from history was a
commonplace or (what is much the same thing) when continued Jewish presence was considered either an uncanny or a
wonderful mystery. To say that the creative and corrective
work of thought about Jewishness and the West that has
taken place since World War II has merely placed the Jews
back into history is less confusing, but it says too little: for
what is distinctive about cultures of diaspora is, in large part,
the way that they deny the progressive or linear rubrics of
secular historiography.

This book was born from our conviction that the cultural
strategies of Jewish diaspora—of regeneration through state-
lessness—speak well (if only the translators are present and
adept) to the dilemmas and the possibilities of the "new diasporas" born in the midst and in the aftermath of the modern

world-system. Our particular interest, as students of human identity and not just of Jewishness, in the range of new diasporas stems in turn from our conviction that strategies of cultural and political identity grounded in exclusive control of territory are ultimately destructive and are both ecologically and technologically doomed.

Nevertheless, we do not believe that the motion and evanescent freedoms of postmodernity give rise, finally and at least, to the era of the emancipated individual. True, the forms and the modes of social connection—both around the planet in the present and anamnestically, with ancestors inherited and adopted—shift with fearsome rapidity; languages die in the mouths of their speakers and are reborn, fragmented, as links in the Web. All the more reason, all the more urgency for a work always bearing a measure of recuperation and a measure of critique. Here is the meat of our culture, here is how our fathers and mothers sustained themselves, constrained each other in loyalty to a shared name, brought forward that name, bestowed it, without your will, upon you.

The book consists of a programmatic introduction and two historically grounded case studies. The introduction, by Jonathan, entitled "Powers of Diaspora," is a cartographic sketch (necessarily inadequate and, by that very token, absolutely intended as a fervent invitation for others to join in completion) of some of the major tropes of Jewish diaspora and how they might be articulated with studies of other new diasporas today. The first of the case studies (by Daniel) is based on Talmudic texts and mobilizes cultural poetic reading strategies. Growing out of the research and thinking of the author for his monograph *Unheroic Conduct* (1997), it adds to the work in that book by developing the specifically political implications of the analysis of rabbinic gendering done there. It explores passages in the Talmud and other core texts of Jewish diaspora that relate how the Rabbis resisted dominant Roman modes of masculinity, thus engendering new texts and refiguring the disparate powers of gender within

Jewish communities. The second case study deals with the contemporary phenomenon of modern American diaspora Jewish politics and uses critical legal theory as its primary research paradigm. Jonathan's "Circumscribing Constitutional Identities in *Kiryas Joel*" brings us full circle to a very local politics of diaspora in confrontation with the jurisprudential rhetoric of the liberal constitutional state. Although the book is written in two separate voices, the voices are close enough together in sensibility and politics (if not always in style) that we have allowed them to merge into a rhetorical "we."

Let these chapters, then, set up echoes both sympathetic and contradictory among themselves, and may this book help us to think further what the shared word "diaspora" can do. For if a lost Jerusalem imagined through a lost Córdoba imagined through a lost Suriname is diaspora to the third power, so is a stolen Africa sung as a lost Zion in Jamaican rhythms on the sidewalks of Eastern Parkway. To say as much as that is, we hope, to catch a lucid glimpse of how creative the powers of diaspora could be.

Introduction

Powers of Diaspora

In the midst of an extended exposition on the genealogical principle in the West, Pierre Legendre presents the following definition of humanity: "Man is 'What is?'" (1985, 76). What could this possibly mean? Let us look at the source cited by Legendre, an excerpt from the Babylonian Talmud:

> Rabbi Yoḥanan said in the name of Rabbi Eleʿazar son of Rabbi Simeon, Wherever you find the words of R. Eleʿazar the son of Rabbi Yose the Galilean in an *Aggadah* make your ear like a funnel. [For he said, It is written,] *It is not because you were greater than any people that the Lord set His love upon you and chose you.* The Holy One, blessed be He, said to Israel, I love you because even when I bestow greatness upon you, you humble yourselves before me. I bestowed greatness upon Abraham, yet he said to Me, *I am but dust and ashes,* upon Moses and Aaron, yet they said, *And I am nothing,* upon David, yet he said, *But I am a worm and no man.* But with the heathens it is not so. I bestowed greatness upon Nimrod, and he said, *Come, let us build us a city;* upon Pharoah, and he said, *Who is the Lord?*; upon Sennacherib,

and he said, *Who are they among all the gods of the countries?*; upon Nebuchadnezzar, and he said, *I will ascend above the heights of the clouds*; upon Hiram king of Tyre, and he said, *I sit in the seat of God, in the heart of the seas.*

Raba, others say Rabbi Yoḥanan said, More significant is that which is said of Moses and Aaron than that which is said of Abraham. Of Abraham it is said, *I am but dust and ashes,* whereas of Moses and Aaron it is said, *And we are nothing.*

Raba, others say Rabbi Yoḥanan also said, The world exists only on account of [the merit of] Moses and Aaron, for it is written here, *And we are nothing,* and it is written there [of the world], *He hangeth the earth upon nothing.* (Babylonian Talmud, Ḥullin 89a)

Let us try to make our ears like funnels; let us hear this story well. Keep in mind the chain of authorities through whom it comes to us. A named Rabbi invokes one Eleʿazar, identified by his paternity, as the source of a saying of a different Eleʿazar, with a different paternity.

Taken as a whole, the passage seems yet another reminder to Israel that it has a special relationship with God, and that this special relationship initially has more to do with God than with Israel. Israel depends and responds. Yet the way in which Israel characteristically responds confirms the wisdom of God's choice. The Rabbis are praising the greatness of Israel's humility and, perhaps, reminding Israel that humility is its strong point. Another way of putting this might be: the Rabbis suggest that in recognizing the significance of nothingness, Israel has access to a different, more profound, and elemental wisdom. At the same time, of course, the story necessarily tells a joke on itself, undercutting Israel's pious claims to humility by loudly proclaiming how humble we are.

Israel's typical stance before God is contrasted here to that of various paragons of the idolaters, the gentiles, each of whom refuses to recognize the God who instilled greatness on him. Pharaoh denies God's existence. Sennacherib suggests that he is a God like any other. Nebuchadnezzar aspires to divine heights. Hiram claims to occupy the divine place. Less obvious, perhaps, is the offense of Nimrod, choosing to use the power bestowed upon him to fix the place for "us," a city whose boundaries will be that of "us." Endowed with greatness, the gentile paragons typically deny the Bestower and solipsistically project themselves in space. They exult in presence, taking power to be an attribute of themselves.

Not so Israel's paragons, Abraham, the brother team of Moses and Aaron, and David. Yet these three examples are not equal in humility. Notice that David appears only in the first-round citation of Israel's great moments of humility. Why is it that his "I am a worm and no man" does not bear another citation in this text? Perhaps because he was, after all, a king; perhaps because the overt denial of his own humanity transgresses the limits of decent self-abasement.

Or maybe the story simply requires an initial third figure, then to be rejected. In this respect the rabbinic version recalls the later folk version of Yiddish-speaking Jewry, which may or may not be directly rooted in the Talmudic text: A congregation has reached the emotional high point of the Yom Kippur ritual. It is just before sundown at the end of the fast, the time of the Neʿilah service when the gates of mercy are about to close before souls are judged for the year to come. In a transport of penitence, the rabbi flings himself to the floor and cries out, "Lord, I am nothing!" The cantor beside him, caught up in the same moment, likewise prostrates himself and cries out, "Lord, I am nothing!" The sexton, seeing this, falls down and shouts, "Lord, I am nothing," upon which the rabbi and the cantor look at each other and say, "Look who thinks he's nothing!"

In any event David is eliminated. Abraham compares himself to the dust of the earth from which, it is said, man is made, while Moses and Aaron ask the question, "We are—what?" The Hebrew words, *naḥnu ma,* are interpreted by Raba (or Rabbi Yoḥanan) as "we are nothing." Is this reading merely an attempt to make a didactic point about the importance of humility, allowing the punch line, "He hangs the earth upon nothing" *(beli-ma)*? Not quite, for this latter citation itself depends upon a highly contingent reading of the word *beli-ma* as "without anything."

Ma thus means the interrogatory "what?" and the substantive "nothing." It also equals *beli-ma,* "not-what," "without anything." At this point we are back where we started, with Legendre's cryptic aphorism, "Man is 'What is?'" It is not enough to *identify* ourselves as worms or even as the dust from which we spring; abasement without more doesn't get us very far. Like the rabbi and the cantor (and unlike the poor sexton), you have to be something in order to be nothing. Not everyone can acknowledge nothingness. Whatever we are is founded on an acknowledgment of absence, or lack. Upon this question we found ourselves.

The Talmudic passage, which begins by reminding us that Israel was not chosen for greatness, thus concludes by identifying Israel's true greatness. We remind ourselves of what we are by reminding ourselves of what we miss, of the "without anything" on which the earth depends. Whenever this wisdom threatens to blind us, we are in danger of losing it. We simultaneously tell the stories of our specialness and remind ourselves how risky those stories are. We sustain the wisdom by embodying and reiterating the question, *"naḥnu ma,"* we are—what is?

This is the paradoxical power of diaspora. On the one hand, everything that defines us is compounded of all the questions of our ancestors. On the other hand, everything is permanently at risk. Thus contingency and genealogy are the two central components of diasporic consciousness.

The particular shape that the investigation "We are what?" is to take in this book is determined by a remarkable turn in world culture. For the modern understanding, the Jewish question had to do with understanding Israel's place among the nations. What was to be done with this diaspora that

threatened, that constantly questioned the very attempt to organize the world polity as a neatly bounded set of so many
defined, autonomous centers—the attempt to realize what
was called the nation-state system? After fifty years of experience with the tortured contradictions of the "Jewish state," it
is time to ask the new question of Israel's "place" among the
diasporas.

As always for us, the question is found at a narrow but
fruitful place between a reified collective identity and a rari-
fied critical individualism. We ask the question because that is
how we imagine ourselves being, once again or still, Jewish;
we seek that place because we also want to recognize ourselves in you. That, at any rate, is our claim on your attention, for our account here is not meant to be nostalgic salvage
of the innocent picturesque. The particular may or may not
have a claim to protection, but by itself (and by definition) it
is not of general significance. "The 'local' is of no real interest
except where it allows a better grasp, by virtue of proximity,
of the interaction between the abstract and the concrete, between experience and the universal, between the individual
and the collective" (Mattelart 1994, 198).[1]

Diaspora, partaking always of the local, but by definition
never confined to it, thus suggests itself as a place where that
interaction can be grasped. This suggests in turn that there
may be something to be gained from thinking about diaspora
not merely as a comparative social or historical phenomenon,
not even only as a predicament shared by many people or
peoples who otherwise have little else in common, but as a
positive *resource* in the necessary rethinking of models of
polity in the current erosion and questioning of the modern
nation-state system and ideal.

One of those issues that should be borne in mind throughout this introduction is the suggestion that a critical privileging
of diaspora—that is, taking diaspora provisionally as a "normal" situation rather than a negative symptom of disorder—
will first of all help us to identify, if not immediately overturn,

a number of liberal assumptions about the appropriate goal of social scholarship and the "normal" bounds of polity.[2] Thus, for example, Michael Walzer suggests a "territorial or locational right" to citizenship, rooted in the preexisting relation between nations and countries, since "the link between people and land is a crucial feature of national identity" (1983, 43–44). Walzer is consistent in adding that these democratic rights cannot be limited arbitrarily but "must be open to all those who live within [the state's] territory, work in the local economy, and are subject to local laws" (60).[3] Somewhat similarly, K. Anthony Appiah naturalizes the links between cultures and states by claiming that "nations never preexist states" (1997, 623).

Not all liberal theorists so thoroughly identify political rights with territoriality per se. Bruce Ackerman, for example, stresses dialogic participation as the criterion for citizenship and, consistent with that stress, insists that the only justification for limiting immigration "is to protect the ongoing process of liberal conversation itself" (1980, 95). Yet Ackerman, too, assumes that citizenship is to be had within a state, territorially defined. To insist once again that the state and its affective association with a certain polity are made, not given— that this "production of a normative conception that links authority, territory, [and] population . . . entails a great deal of hard work on the part of statespersons, diplomats, and intellectuals" (Biersteker and Weber 1996, 3)—does not of course delegitimize the state. Even those normatively devoted to the ideal of the liberal state may and should acknowledge that it is a *project*.[4] Yet this reminder of its contingency should also make room for the exploration of alternatives. Nor need the alternatives be stark: we may ultimately wish to think of allocating rights, obligations, and authority among states, persons, and organizations according to criteria other than those separating the state from civil society.[5]

This book is therefore an argument *for* diaspora, and at the same time an attempt to identify and avoid at least some of the risks inherent in promoting "diaspora" as a new catch-word in the global theorization of diversity. In recent years scholars have found the term congenial as a way to describe cultural formations as diverse as the Chicano/a disruption of the U.S.-Mexico border, the Black Atlantic, the overseas Chinese, and intellectuals from the Indian subcontinent living and working inside the Euro-American metropole.[6] Noting this expansion of the term will bring us to the issue of whether diaspora is "objectively" an increasing phenomenon in the latest "time-space compression" (Harvey 1989) and/or whether (as suggested in J. Boyarin 1994) this technological or political-economic phenomenon of greater and more transitory movements of population is powerfully linked to the simultaneous collapse of time and space as distinct, objective vectors of experience on the one hand, and of the anamnestic and territorial boundaries of the nation on the other hand.

This broadened deployment of the concept offers rich material for a reinvigoration of Jewish thought. Yet the converse is also true: analyses of non-Jewish diasporas will be most fruitful when they engage in dialogue with the specific Jewish context in which the term originated. At the same time, attention must be paid to the powers exercised "within" diasporic communities. Not only celebration but also critique of those internal powers is needed. Evaluating diaspora entails acknowledging the ways that such identity is maintained through exclusion and oppression of internal others (especially women) and external others.

Thus it will not answer to assert that diasporic communities exert the powers available to them exclusively in an *oppositional* mode, along the lines of one recent account that designates as "third time-spaces" something like what we are calling powers of diaspora. In this account, "third time-spaces paradoxically do practice their own arbitrary provisional closures, in order to enact agency toward dismantling the Eurocenter, or to enable identity politics beyond the reactive mode" (Lavie and Swedenburg 1996, 17). This is necessarily and tautologically true if all of the cultural "spaces" being considered are tested and precertified by the criterion of opposition to some presumed center, but it is not clear that opposition exhausts the motivations of diasporic communities. More "selfish" reasons—preservation of lives or of identities for their own sake, without regard to any external measure of their worth—come into play equally often.

The same account also includes, however, a statement closer to the sensibility we are reaching for here, imbued with the contingency of diasporic existence and diasporic criticism:

> As identity and place are forced into constantly shifting configurations of partial overlap, their ragged edges cannot be smoothed out. Identity and place perpetually create both new outer borders, where no imbrication has occurred, and inner borders, between the areas of overlay and the vestigial spaces of nonoverlay. The grating that results from their forced combination sparks inchoate energies that mobilize and activate the agency of coalition politics. (Lavie and Swedenburg 1996, 18)

Here again, however, it must be said that not only "coalition politics" are mobilized and activated. The ragged edges between diasporas sometimes spark violence rather than, or in addition to, coalition politics, as in the case of tensions between Lubavitch Hasidic Jews and members of the African diaspora in Crown Heights, Brooklyn. The powers of diaspora are not necessarily benign, whether directed outward or inward.

An investigation of the powers of diaspora is thus vitiated by a hasty assumption that such powers are only creative or progressive. Nor should this discussion pass without any acknowledgment that diaspora is also always a situation of risk, as often as not a situation of danger. Bearing the danger in mind may somewhat alleviate the risk of overgeneralizing from a selective concentration on those diasporic situations where various populations enjoy both relative autonomy and a high degree of cultural permeability vis-à-vis the "host" majority or other groups.

A brief glance at a globe (from its earlier sense referring to "the world," the term has come to mean a small spherical representation of the earth) confirms the truism at the heart of critical geography, that territorialist nation-statism is the hegemonic modern mode of polity (e.g., Portugali 1988). As the very term "state" implies, nation-statism as a global and universal logic seeks to fix ethnically (genealogically and culturally) homogeneous human groups within nonoverlapping, neatly bounded, and permanent geographical boundaries. It is this neat mapping of nations onto nonoverlapping and unique global spaces that the powers of diaspora confront, by which they are manipulated, and which they manipulate in their turn (Shain 1994). Indeed the *interaction* between diasporic populations and national governments is a theme that cannot be dismissed in any thorough study of the powers of diaspora, especially since the analysis of nation-states themselves fails wherever it neglects the role and control of diasporas in the very constitution of the nation-state. States made up of immigrant groups and dispossessed indigenous groups, such as the United States, Israel, or Australia, seek usually to meld their disparate constituencies into one permanent and homogeneous nation (Goldberg 1977; Kapferer 1988); others, as in Trinidad, seek to freeze the constituent groups as a timeless "mosaic" of distinct and impermeable ethnicities (Segal 1994). Nevertheless, this interaction will receive short shrift in this preliminary attempt to sketch out the potentials and pitfalls of the diasporic *model,* an attempt that derives from an implicit and as yet vague projection in which not merely do diasporas interact with nation-states, but global polity per se is perpetually organized, disorganized, and reorganized according to logics of diaspora.

Diaspora is *not* equivalent to pluralism or internationalism. It is egocentric. These latter are more the complements than the alternatives or correctives to nationalism. Pluralism (which cannot be dismissed as long as the nation-state remains the dominant form of organization) reduces incommensurate differences to equivalent shades upon a single palette. Much as certain universalizing forms of antiracism share underlying premises with racism (Balibar 1990), internationalism falls within the same logic as nationalism, both seeing the ethnic, territorial nation as the proper *unit* of polity and collective identity—differing only on whether the normal state of relations between those units is one of conflict or potential harmony. In fact, since the most common form of encounter between people "identified" with different nations is in the context of immigration and all of its attendant mistakes and uncertainties, an ideology that at least implicitly asserts that people should be judged as representatives of their nation inevitably produces stigmatization and failures (Malkki 1994).

Diaspora offers an alternative "ground" to that of the territorial state for the intricate and always contentious linkage between cultural identity and political organization. Such an alternative ground could avoid the necessarily violent ways in which states resist their own inevitable impermanence. It could also ameliorate the insistence on purity that derives from the dominant, static conception of legitimate collective identity. This alternative ground could also afford greater cultural-political "time-space" for the continued existence of established diasporic communities and for the inevitable emergence and elaboration of new diasporas in the transnational cultural and economic sphere. That, at any rate, is the most general notion of the powers of diaspora that we want to propose.

Any possibility of linking this projective notion of diaspora as a resource in response to the legitimation crisis of the nation-state will be vitiated if the term "diaspora" is discussed in a fashion completely removed from its formative historical and ethnic framework. It is important to insist not on the *centrality* of Jewish diaspora nor on its *logical priority* within comparative diaspora studies, but on the need to refer to, and better understand, Jewish diaspora history within the contemporary diasporic rubric. Doing so promises, first of all, to contribute to the reinvention of Jewish studies by finding points of intersection between studies in Jewish culture and those cultures that are already vibrantly located within critical cultural studies. But even more so, if Jewish diaspora is confined to the archives—either as already sufficiently researched and acknowledged (having nothing to teach postcolonial studies), or worse yet, as *obviated* because there is now, after all, a Jewish state—key considerations in comparative diaspora studies will not be articulated.

Beyond its sheer antiquity, Jewish diaspora might still be regarded as the most precise or concentrated diasporic experience, in several respects. One of these is the persistence of Jewish communities, not only outside the homeland, and not only in the absence of political hegemony enjoyed by fellows in the homeland, but, for centuries, in the absence even of a substantial community of fellows actually living in the homeland, such that the Jewish diasporic relation *to the homeland* (rather than the relation of its various branches to each other) is primarily commemorative, rather than kin-based or economic. Another distinctive feature of Jewish diaspora is the repeated experience of *rediasporization*. This results in a situation where, to borrow a term from Homi Bhabha, the imaginary Jewish homeland is "less than one and double" (1994): Zion longed for and imagined through Cordoba, Cairo, or Vilna, and these frequently palimpsested one on the other such that Cairo becomes a remembered Cordoba and the new Jerusalem a remembered Vilna. Within this process of repeated removal and regrounding, Jewish culture has elaborated a range of absolutely indispensable technologies of cultural transformation (such as modeling of commemorations for newer collective losses, the way Lamentations mourns the loss of the Temple [see A. Mintz 1984]; or the use of precedent and hermeneutics in rabbinic law to articulate workable and authoritative responses to dilemmas encountered for the first time by "the tradition"; or, famously, the centrality of public reading of the Bible in the formation and replication of the Jewish "textual community" [see Stock 1990]), all of which taken together have afforded Jewishness the paradoxic power of *nakhnu-ma,* survival and presence through absence and loss.

A quick glance at the differential situating of the rubric of diaspora vis-à-vis particular groups in three articles written between 1931 and 1994 suggests a displacement of the automatic association of "Jews" with "diaspora"—or we might say, a shift from "*the* diaspora" to "diasporas." Significantly, the article on "Diaspora" in the earlier *Encyclopaedia of the Social Sciences* is the contribution of the great synthesizing Jewish historian and secular, nonterritorial Yiddish nationalist Simon Dubnow. Dubnow's article starts by mentioning "Magna Graecia" as "a Greek diaspora in the ancient Roman Empire," immediately adding that "a typical case of diaspora is presented by the Armenians" (1931, 126), yet the bulk of his discussion documents the progression of Jewish communities outside Palestine. By the early 1980s, the anthropologist Elliot Skinner regards Jews as the paradigm but pays detailed attention to a number of other examples, including his primary comparison with the African diaspora (1982). Most recently the cultural historian and critic James Clifford is wary of *centering* the term around its specifically Jewish associations, wary of "running the risk of making Jewish experience again the normative model" (1994, 324). In a different register, then, we might speak about concentric "powers" of diaspora as the different levels of abstraction and generalization by which the term's dimensions are multiplied. We may run the risk of a situation in which how far "diaspora" has been displaced from Jewish references is taken as an indication of the extent to which the term has been rendered theoretically sublime.

Thus a published statement by Stuart Hall is explicitly exclusive and dismissive of the Jewish experience of diaspora—and grossly distorted to boot:

The "New World" presence—America, *Terra Incognita*—is therefore itself the beginning of diaspora, of diversity, of hy-

bridity and difference, what makes Afro-Caribbean people already people of a diaspora. I use this term here metaphorically, not literally: diaspora does not refer us to those scattered
tribes whose identity can only be secured in relation to some
sacred homeland to which they must at all costs return, even
if it means pushing other people into the sea. This is the old,
the imperialising, the hegemonising, form of "ethnicity." We
have seen the fate of the people of Palestine at the hands of
this backward-looking conception of diaspora—and the complicity of the West with it. The diaspora experience as I intend
it here is defined, not by essence or purity, but by the recognition of a necessary heterogeneity; by a conception of "identity" which lives with and through, not despite, difference; by
hybridity. (1990, 235)

Here Hall celebrates "newness" per se as if he were utterly unaware of the Benjaminian critique of the complicity between
progress and imperialism. Thus he actually assumes a blithely
poetic Old World–centric perspective, celebrating the New
World as a space of free self-creation and canceling out the
prior presence of native peoples to whom the land was hardly
terra incognita. He identifies Jewishness *only* with a lack,
a neurotic attachment to the lost homeland. Hall identifies
Zionism—the attempt to *negate* Jewish diasporic existence—
with Jewish diasporism; when Jewishness is reduced to a caricatured Zionism in this fashion, it is indeed the case that
anti-Zionism is anti-Judaism. He confuses the standard fear,
endlessly reiterated in Zionist rhetoric, that the Arabs will
"push the Jews into the sea" with an implicit claim that this is
what the Zionists did to the Palestinians. In effect, he banishes Jews from the brave new world of hybridity. Hall's hybridity, as it would appear from this quote, must be purified—
of Jews. More could be said about the multiple, profound,
and vicious ironies in this quote, but this should suffice to reinforce our point about the dangers of attempting to "transcend" Jewishness in cultural studies of the new diasporas.

A few years later, Vijay Mishra, a professor of English and comparative literature at Murdoch University in Perth, Australia, described his recent research in the newsletter of the Center for Cultural Studies at the University of California at Santa Cruz as follows:

> My research at the Center for Cultural Studies will focus on the literature of the Indian diaspora in the undertheorized field of "diasporology" generally. The OED (Oxford English Dictionary) defines the word diaspora as "dispersion" and cites examples only of Jewish diaspora. I would want to use the term diaspora as follows:
>
> 1. Relatively homogeneous, displaced communities brought to serve the Empire . . .
>
> 2. Emerging new diasporas based on free migration linked to late, modern capitalism . . .
>
> 3. Any group of migrants that considers itself to be on the periphery of power, or excluded from sharing power. (1994)

This is a significant resituation of the range of experiences that are to be considered under the term "diaspora." We are concerned that it not be read in a way that could exclude Jewish experience by transcending or "superseding" the reference to Jews, following a rhetoric analogous to that used by early Christian writers to situate their own relation to Jewishness (see J. Boyarin 1992 and 1994). Not that we would want in any way to impede a move to recast diaspora away from a presumptively Western or Eurocentric focus. But if the references to Jews are abandoned, vital insights about the ways continued Jewish existence has *always* troubled the presumptions of the Christian West to stable centrality might still be lost, and the tendency to see Jews only as a certain kind of marginal Europeans may be reinforced. Encouragingly, the results of Mishra's own research indicate a nuanced understanding of the poetics of Jewish diaspora, its continued value "to situate and critique the imaginary construction of a homeland as the central *mythomateur* of diaspora histories," and the profound disjuncture between Zionism and traditional Jewish diaspora identity (1996, 425).

It must quickly be noted that merely acknowledging the Jewish context in which the term "diaspora" first appears does not guarantee particular insights into other diasporas or even into the Jewish diaspora. Thus Skinner notes well that the concept of diaspora "derives from the historic experience of the Jewish people" (1982, 11), but only *after* a summary paragraph implicitly assuming that diasporic populations remain in complex relation with a population remaining "at home." More tellingly perhaps, Skinner's effort at setting out comparisons between African and Jewish diasporas is flawed by the assertion that like Africans taken into New World slavery, the Jewish diaspora was primarily constituted by external coercion (13), as well as by his linked assumption that Jewish diaspora is in essence an overarching condition of oppression and that "restitution" of the homeland in the formation of the Jewish state of Israel was in itself good for the collective (16). Skinner generally assumes that homeland-*states* want to serve as guarantors of diasporic security and do so effectively (36). For Skinner, the natural options in a situation where a diasporic population is *not* powerless or oppressed tend either in the direction of successful assimilation to the "host" population or to repatriation, but not to the perpetuation of diasporic community. Skinner notes and discusses extensively the fact that in most cases where diasporic populations have an opportunity to "return" en masse, they fail to do so. He sees this as "a major dialectical contradiction" (19), but of course this is so only if one takes the territorial ethnic-state as an a priori norm. For Skinner this results in the claim that the existence of a Jewish state makes it actually more difficult "for persons to be *Jews* and remain in the diaspora," and in the odd prediction that "American and other Jews may have to choose either Israeli citizenship or the citizenship of the state in which they were born or live" (32).[7] This ominous vision returns, of course, to Skinner's assumption that diaspora is an inherently unstable and undesirable situation vis-à-vis the "normal" coincidence of citizenship and identity. In short, Skinner does not acknowledge the powers of diaspora.

Within the realm of cultural politics, one of the key powers of diaspora consists in being recognized as one of the diasporas that must be taken into consideration. Which diasporas are privileged (in that precise sense) today?[8] Certainly the Indian diaspora is one of them (see, for example, Nandy 1990, 103). This may be traced in great part to the astonishing number of leading humanities scholars and social scientists who are from or still in the subcontinent, which in turn has something to do with the extraordinary combination of post-colonial identity and thorough English education. It is no accident that Homi Bhabha and Gayatri Spivak, two of the figures who have done the most to make questions of interference between "Indian" postcoloniality and "Western" critical modernity a key topos of theory, are professors of English. Both of these scholars, furthermore, are thoroughly aware of the constitutive irony in the fact that theories of marginality are often propounded at or near the center (see, for example, Spivak 1989). The powerful access to English enjoyed by many scholars of Indian origin should not be traced solely to the vagaries of English colonial policy, however, but to the linguistic adaptability of Indian diasporic communities as well (see Ghosh 1989).

That adaptibility may be related in turn to the heterogeneity (including linguistic) of India itself. Keya Ganguly thus notes that "the diverse and heteroglossic nature of subcontinental groups does not lend itself to easy assimilation under a par-ticular 'tradition'" (1992, 43). At the same time, she does not want merely to expose the idea of an overarching Indian iden-tity in diaspora as illusory: "it is crucial to think about the significance of *names* in the construction of identity" (48; em-phasis added). The paradox between the cultural diversity of the subcontinent, and the powerful operations of the name

"India" *especially* outside the subcontinent, may be another key to the extraordinary creativity of this diaspora.

In any case, a sustained effort at dialogue and comparison between and among subcontinent and Jewish diaspora scholars would seem to be a richly promising project. One of the precise and yet resonant foci of such a conversation might be the ways that the term "diaspora" is actually embedded in those discourses through which the various group identities are transformed, maintained, or dissipated. There seems to be a transvaluation of that which is understood commonsensically as the Jewish "diaspora," articulated not only among critical Jewish intellectuals outside the institutional mainstream but within the very institutional core that, for the last fifty years, has assumed its own role to be largely that of support for the "renewed, vital and real Jewish present and future" represented by the state of Israel. How do such expressions articulate with the cultural studies or critical theory use of the term "diaspora"? What comparable notes might begin to be made about the politics of the term *within* (to the extent, that is, that there are such boundaries between "internal" and "external" discourse of diasporic groups) the Indian diaspora? How do its English professors relate to its physicians and its business-people? Ganguly notes parenthetically, "I have often been taken to task for questioning things that are supposed to be inviolable; but in the end, my opinions do not count for much since I am generally regarded as a radical intellectual" (1992, 44). Yet, given that much of her analysis centers on the semi-deliberate, semiconscious structuring of accounts of authenticity, authority, and domesticity within the Indian diasporic community, why should she be so readily dismissive of the suggestion that she may have been "heard" by her interlocutors in ways that they could not acknowledge at the time? This very interrogation of the placement of the concept of diaspora within various diasporic-communal[9] discourses is at the same time a test case for the tensions of dialogic openness versus ideological unity within diasporic groups.

Other diasporic identities that have not yet been brought fully within the emerging discourse of comparative diasporas present questions of insiderhood/outsiderhood, or tensions between discourse and actuality, that have only begun to be explored within the interdisciplinary cultural studies frame. For a group like the Rom (unlike South Asians or Jews), even the work that is done and recognized within the academy is not usually signed by those who identify personally with the collective identity. But the work of inviting the Gypsies, so to speak, has certainly begun. For example, in an extraordinarily rich essay on "The Time of the Gypsies," Katie Trumpener has laid out a number of ways in which both the figure of the Gypsy in European culture and the constrained social spaces in which the peoples called "Gypsies" continue to live belong within the agenda of studies in diaspora. I will content myself here with underscoring her point that non-Rom appear unwilling to surrender or question the myths *about* Rom by which they have constructed their own identities, even to an extent that would widen the social space for Romani life in the present to a tolerable level (1992). Yet this should be understood as more than a plea for tolerance. Repressive stereotyping of the other often serves, more than anything, to paper over poorly constructed aspects of a collective self. Thus a more sustained questioning of these images of diasporic peoples that help to constitute presumptively "stable" dominant identities would potentially afford a greater openness and transparency within the dominant identities themselves.

Less clear in Trumpener's account is a problem that the Rom also raise in a very sharp form. This is the question of a diasporist notion of polity. Presumably, in order for diasporic groups to be effective polities, they need or would need to adopt some of the basic strictures of unique, nonoverlapping, and encompassing identity, simultaneously cultural and political, that characterize the nation-statist rationales that we are trying to criticize and in part replace through focusing on diaspora itself. To what extent are, in fact, diasporic communities legal communities?

The legal scholars Walter Weyrauch and Maureen Ann Bell have explored this question in the case of the Rom. Their article begins by drawing a distinction between "State Law vs. Private Lawmaking" (326, 373ff.). Although they progressively minimize this distinction, reaching toward a "perspective [in which] the dichotomy between private lawmaking and the law of the state disappears" (395), note that the state retains categorical priority. Weyrauch and Bell focus generally on how "Gypsy law has evolved to insulate Gypsies from the host society, and thus to maintain its own insularity from the host legal system" (340). Their discussion of the way Romani law serves this insulating function is focused on the concept of *marime,* which

> has a dual meaning: it refers both to a state of pollution as well as to the sentence of expulsion imposed for violation of purity rules or any behavior disruptive to the Gypsy community. (342)

In other respects as well, including the distribution of exclusive business rights within specific territories (355) and the strategic use of the in-group language to create cultural advantages in dealings with outsiders (365), Rom exhibit carefully maintained characteristics common to Jews and other diasporic groups.

By publishing an extended study of Romani law in a major law journal, Weyrauch and Bell take a significant step toward greater recognition of the powers of diaspora. They err, however, in assuming that these techniques for group maintenance are to be understood as a search for the greatest degree of isolation possible, and that their relative success is to be evaluated on such terms (397). Whether or not Rom or others sometimes speak in such terms, purity is not the only goal of diasporic communities. Nor is autonomy to be confused with the *absence* of nomos.[10]

In a response to Weyrauch and Bell, Michael Reisman describes their essay as addressing "an acute problem that contemporary democracies are only beginning to address systematically: how a society should relate to smaller autonomous communities within its borders" (1993, 402). Ironically, the very designation of any group as autonomous is a designation from outside, not inside. Reisman's reference infra to "autonomous" groups within the Ottoman Empire gets this right, since the Ottoman rulers designated religious minority groups as autonomous:

> Under the *millet* system, the Osmanlis granted a high degree
> of autonomy to individual communities, each of which could
> organize and manage itself legally and politically under autonomous institutions and leadership. (414)

"Autonomy" was "granted." It never exists in isolation. In this sense, Reisman is again correct to insist that "[i]n an interdependent, global industrial and science-based civilization, no group is truly autonomous" (415). His alternative, however, to Ottoman-style recognition of group autonomy rights is a questionable one:

> The rights of group formation and the tolerated authority of
> group elites over their members extend insofar as they are indispensable for the achievement of individual rights. They
> cannot be justified if their effect is to abridge or limit basic individual rights. (416)

Unfortunately this reassertion of the universal rights of man is not coherent. It relies on a bare assertion, a *profession de foi* in the existence of some set of "basic individual rights," which can be objectively identified and which are susceptible to protection through an institutionalized procedure for hearing claims of infringement *because* individuals are "entitled" to make those claims. It furthermore assumes that in some way rights-bearing individuals can always be distinguished from the groups to which they adhere or from which they separate themselves. It effectively limits group autonomy to the realm of associations voluntarily entered into by autonomous, that is, adult, individuals. Strictly enforced, it would probably demand a much greater intrusion by the State into the structure of numerous communities in the United States than currently obtains.

On the other hand, observing that autonomy is not to be confused with the lack of nomos, and that diasporic communities have their own means of enforcement, reminds us that diasporic claims for legitimation and identity seem to demand a rhetoric of unity[11] (how strong could a claim to represent "various people called Gypsies all over Europe" [Malkki 1994, 56] be?). This monolithic rhetoric in turn undercuts the transvaluation of fragmentation and contingency that are a chief power of diaspora in critical discussions of identity.

The historical experience and political program of the nineteenth- and early-twentieth-century Jewish Worker's Bund in Russia, Poland, and Lithuania also evidence this dilemma. This movement of intellectuals and workers was a secular-nationalist organization that argued for the organization of socialist struggle through the coordination of autonomous ethnic organizations and for the organization of education and culture on lines of nationality—that is, separate and autonomous schools, newspapers, theaters, and so forth for Jews, Ukrainians, Russians, and any other national group that might be recognized within a socialist state. In the event, Lenin's faction in the Russian Social Democratic Party refused to accept the Bundist program for national-cultural autonomy when it was proposed at the Second Party Congress in 1903. This event may be analyzed both as a moment in, and as a key precipitant of, the persistent failure of the European left to acknowledge the power of nonterritorial, non-state-based collective identities. It ultimately reinforced the hegemony of territorialist, Romantic, liberal nation-statism in modern Europe and the eventual hegemony of Zionism in Jewish politics in the second half of the twentieth century.

Not that the Bundist program may be retrospectively judged unproblematically correct. In effect such a program—quite precisely *multicultural*—required every citizen to declare her or his nationality. This policy was in turn adopted by the Bolsheviks (with different purposes, but to a large extent following the same rationale), and with consequences ultimately seen as generally discriminatory by those concerned with Jewish life in the Soviet Union. The dilemma presented by the Bund's program, then, may be described as an impossible choice between a failure to recognize group rights and autonomy on the one hand, and constrictive external definition on the other. To the extent liberal states such as England, France, and the United States have attempted to institutionalize multiculturalist pluralism since World War II, the same problem arises. In a different register—one with obvious and immediate consequences for far fewer lives—a similar dilemma is presented by the problematic attempt to specify a field of comparative diasporas.

Reference to the Soviet Union raises the further question of diasporas within state boundaries, which is significant for at least two reasons. First of all, especially within "empire states" such as the Soviet Union and the United States, they are a significant phenomenon in themselves, and failure to consider them will leave us with an inadequate notion of the possible dimensions of diaspora. Thus the "Jewish autonomous region" of Birobidjan set up in the eastern Soviet Union in the 1930s, although ultimately unsustainable, is not just a historical curiosity but an important counterexample to the idea that "solutions" to diaspora are always proposed or attempted within the *memorial* homeland. Second and equally important, focusing on diasporas within states is bracing because when we persist in the habit of focusing exclusively on diasporic spread across national borders, we unwittingly reinforce the prejudice toward thinking of those borders as the "real" power divides, the ones that really count.

Thinking of diasporas within states may likewise give us

new ways of thinking through the cultural dynamics of groups such as Native Americans—dynamics that may well include hitherto overlooked instances of the persistence of specific identities. Thus, although the Delaware Indian populations of the East Coast lost their corporate local identity at a relatively early stage in the history of European-Indian encounters, at present there are individuals born and still living west of the Mississippi who identify as Delaware Indians. This is the kind of phenomenon that might seem of merely poetic or anecdotal significance, unless one is already considering the powers of diaspora. Diasporas-within-states might even afford a modestly coherent logic of identification between indigenist and diasporist alternatives, challenges, or subversions of the nation-state. The shared stance—to the side of, moving around the state—may be hinted at through Pierre Clastres's formulation of the political significance of the millennialism of the Tupi-Guarani in Brazil: "Tupi-Guarani prophetism is the heroic attempt of a primitive society to put an end to unhappiness by means of a radical refusal of the One, as the universal essence of the State" (1987, 217, quoted in Goldsmith 1993, 71). The concept of diaspora quite literally, within its own etymology, also contains this refusal of static unity, but an exclusive focus on the diasporic as *transnational* might lead us to assume by contrast a necessary complicity between indigenism and statism.[12]

Here we might begin to bump up against the limits to which the concept of diaspora may plausibly or usefully be stretched. As suggested earlier, we do not want the term to cover everything. The question of the imbalance between a totalizing categorical usage of the term "diaspora" and the discourses within various diasporic formations that may not recognize that category leads us to the necessary recognition that whatever the criterion for judging our own discourse may be, it cannot rest on a simplistic notion of pluralist (different but in the same ways) tolerance—the sort of logic driving the Bund's program at the turn of the twentieth century.

Nor can it demand a *synthetic* account, one that would take account of (and thereby presume to have mastered) every particular diasporic framework.[13]

Another danger, one which Paul Gilroy energetically analyzes in his critique of certain forms of Afrocentrism (1993, 189ff.), is the impulse to mobilize a totalizing antimodernist revisionism in the name of tradition. Diaspora per se is not always validated in tradition; after all, the biblical Hebrew word translated as "diaspora" in the Septuagint might better be translated as "abomination." Similarly, many sources, both Christian and Jewish, take an extremely negative view of "multicultural" ancient Babylon (Goldsmith 1993, 61ff.). Against this, of course, there are recuperable moments, in premodern Jewish culture at least, where rhetoric is produced suggesting that the lost homeland may, at least provisionally, be well compensated for here and now:

> Isaiah 2:3 reads, "Out of Zion shall go forth the law, and the word of the Lord from Jerusalem," and the theoretical primacy of Jerusalem calls forth no doubts among the celebrated scholars. But when Bari and Otranto, in southern Italy, became established centers of Jewish learning, Rabenu Tam in his *Sefer hayashar* calmly wrote, "For out of Bari shall go forth the law, and the word of the Lord from Otronto," without fearing it would be construed as a desecration of the sacred. (Weinreich 1980, 228)

If Rabenu Tam was thus willing momentarily to accept Bari instead of Jerusalem, should we not perhaps be wary of a facile fetishization of our own losses? A fundamental divide in the contemporary debate about diaspora lies between an approach that focuses on the anamnestic powers of diaspora, creating ties through memory, and an approach that focuses on the liberatory powers of diaspora as release from monolithic attachment. Certainly one of the dangerous ways in which the term "diaspora" is used as a new theoretical fetish appears in the newest phase of the perpetual reinvention of "the West" through renewed discussions of the problem of identity (on which see Derrida 1992 and the discussion of Derrida's book in J. Boyarin 1996). Thus, in the critical literature occasioned by the Columbus quincentennial, we find flamboyant sentences such as "the West continues its diasporic fantasy, its perpetual odyssey of the mind in search of a lost centre."[14] "Diaspora" then becomes conflated with the drama of the alienated or homeless "soul" whose exile or attempted return, always to some place unproblematically assumed to be *home,* is the model life narrative of the Western *individual.*[15]

As with the allegorized figure of the Jew in many moments of post–World War II Continental theory, when "diaspora" is collapsed into this individualized and spiritualized model, the attempt to create cultural "space" for various diasporic communities—and in the process reveal something about the self-constitution of peoples "at home"—is vitiated by the rather blatant return of a universalizing reference to the "we" who are constituted by our very awareness of nonidentity! Despite this, any power that diaspora may have as a concept cannot fail to engage with this same body of advanced theory. Otherwise, we are left in a generally vacuous framework of social-scientific rhetoric, "comparing" diasporas as if the experiences of such disparate groups really were adequately categorized by a term borrowed from one instance in a Greek translation of the Hebrew Bible.

To this extent it may be inescapable that, as with the language of theory in general (Chaterjee 1990), "diaspora talk" is still discursively centered in the framework of progressive, post-Protestant European reason. Yet critical developments within that same framework also suggest links between the contingency of diasporic experience and the appropriateness of trying to articulate a more contingent epistemology—a way of talking about social experience less dependent on the assumption that "theoretical vocabularies are more or less transparent mediums for representing a ready-made reality outside themselves" (Bartelson 1995, 18). The reference to transparency itself recalls a key tension, inherent in our understanding of language as simultaneously referential and symbolic, between the need for shared information and the need for shared metaphors.[16] Armand Mattelart thus disputes the reductive notion of information as a mere fetish of instrumentalist capitalism:

> Information is life itself, a vital flow for staying in time with the times, hence the permanent conflict between the need for transparency and the maintenance of an image. Hence, as well, the difficulty of going beyond a transparency understood as anything other than the struggle for the legitimacy and credibility of the enterprise by means of communication. But transparency, if one were inclined to dreaming aloud, could turn into a vast questioning of the prevailing model of development and progress. (1994, 220)

At the same time, Mattelart discusses the importance of building transnationality through shared symbols (17).

In this regard it is worthwhile observing that diasporic formations of identity and responsibility are themselves independent of "the prevailing model of development and progress." That is, diaspora certainly interacts with the progressivist and neocolonialist model of development supposed to emanate from an advanced Western center, but diasporic communities predate this particular type of world economic system. On the other hand, diasporas are clearly dependent on shared images (that is, rhetorics of common identity) as well as shared information (knowledge pooled from disparate sources that facilitates survival in conditions of insecurity). Furthermore, this heightened sensitivity to the materiality of images and symbols is not only directed internally, within the diasporic group, but constitutes a means of adaptation. The symbols that diasporic subjects strategically engage signally include stereotypes about themselves. This strategy of manipulating external symbols is documented, for example, in Aihwa Ong's essay tracing "the

agency of Asian subjects as they selectively participate in ori-
entalist discourses encountered on travels through the shifting
discursive terrains of the global economy" (1998, 135).

Likewise, "diaspora" is less and less solely an external category applied to certain groups, and increasingly a category
through which these groups articulate themselves. In the case
of diaspora, failure to consider the weight of the word's particular history leads to the risk of taking diaspora as categori-
cally *new*.[17] Thus, along with the tendency to slip back into a
mode of heroically alienated questing individualism in place
of the messy complications of social diaspora, theoretical/
critical/literary discussions of diaspora may lose much of their
power by their reiteration of a unitary notion of premodern
tradition. This is often expressed as the presumption of an
unproblematic relation to a homeland before the diaspora is
inaugurated. On the one hand, the alternative term "migration" presupposes the permanence of the place moved to, and
hence, so to speak, its "ontological" priority, its greater sub-
stantiality or reality vis-à-vis the situation of diaspora or movement. ("Diaspora," as Clifford explains with appropriate nu-
ance, "demurs from the assumption that a certain destination
will lock in or absorb the newcomers" [1994, 304].) From the
standpoint of territorial states, "migrancy" is an intolerable
situation: people are either "im-migrants" or "e-migrants,"
but in either case there is a crossing of a juridical boundary, a
reclassified jurisdiction. First and foremost, the jurisdiction
pertains to property, of which the original form is understood
to be territory; as Bentham suggested long ago, the right of
property "is that right . . . which has brought to an end the
migratory life of nations" (1975).

On the other hand, the "quest" model for migrancy tends to
assume that the migrant begins from a stable homeland. Thus,
at the beginning of his elegant little book on migrancy, Iain
Chambers refers to the migrant as "Cut off from the homelands of tradition" (1991, 6). "Cut off," we must ask, *when*
and through *what modes of discontinuity*? Is such cutting-off a

one-time event? Is it necessarily an event that coincides with literally, physically shipping out and moving? Chambers's implicit assumption that it is only when an individual leaves a homeland that the process of destabilization begins actually undercuts his attempt to illuminate how migrancy denies the notion of stable origins.

The contemporary philosophical text most richly relevant to the articulation of the powers of diaspora is probably Deleuze and Guattari's *A Thousand Plateaus* (1987). Their concepts of "rhizomal" (that is, nonhierarchical and transversal, as opposed to rooted and genealogical) identifications in sign systems and among persons, and of "nomadology" as a critical epistemic stance, bear quite closely on diaspora.[18] Deleuze and Guattari afford the diaspora theorist numerous troubling and productive engagements.

One such engagement rests in their insistence on shattering the monumentality of theoretical concepts as presumptive (we might say presumptuous) universals. They take language as an example to make this point: "There is no language in itself, nor are there any linguistic universals, only a throng of dialects, patois, slangs, and specialized languages" (Deleuze and Guattari 1987, 7). How does this attempt to dislodge not only the idealist tendency to assume that the exempla derive from the concept, but also the possible privileging of any one example as the "truest" language, work if we substitute "diaspora" for "language"? On one hand, of course, it is bracing: we should not define diaspora such that some are more "diasporic" than others, and we must watch the intellectual trap of speaking as if the concept *produces* the various phenomena, rather than merely helping us *think them together.* Yet the translation breaks down at a certain point. In a cultural-historical sense there *is* a "first" diaspora, that of the Jews, from which the word comes, as discussed above. Thus it is neither surprising nor accidental that the linguistic authority immediately cited by Deleuze and Guattari after this radical statement about language ("Language is, in [Uriel] Weinreich's words, 'an essentially heterogeneous reality'" [ibid.]) was the son and scholarly heir of Max Weinreich, himself the Bundist theorist and historian of Yiddish diaspora culture.

Likewise it seems worthwhile attempting to formulate the dilemma around which this essay centers—the dilemma of the effort to put into practice a "coalitional" politics of diasporic culture, confounded by the very differences it wishes to allow a field for—in terms of a challenge put forth by Deleuze and Guattari, who confront the image of the "root" of natural identity with the alternative metaphor of the interconnected but not "grounded" rhizome. It is easy to see why choosing a different "natural symbol" for the dynamics of identification is attractive: the image of the rhizome submits neither to autonomy nor to essentialism. Could the notion of diaspora similarly be replaced with some metaphor that does not roll us immediately back into the conflict of universals and particulars? Probably not, especially since, as it turns out, the rhizome doesn't quite supplant roots. Deleuze and Guattari seem uneasy about totalizing their nature metaphor when they claim to replace roots with rhizomes: "A rhizome as subterranean stem is absolutely different from roots and radicals" (1987, 6). The image expresses well their insistence on the value of the *horizontal,* of surface connections rather than depth, or, as they put it elsewhere, of contagion rather than filiation (242).[19] Yet the need to assert an "absolute" difference between the rhizome model and that of roots goes against the whole force of their anti-absolutist work. Indeed, Deleuze and Guattari are themselves not above making arguments from the "roots" of words, from their etymologies, as in their assertion that the idea of a nomos originally referred to the dispersion of shepherds across pasturelands (and was hence linked to nomadism, which is their name for a social model opposed to the State) and was contrasted to the Logos of the territorial, bounded city (557, note 51). Furthermore, if we read "homeland" for "root" in this quote from Deleuze and Guattari (a substitution fully authorized by the connotation *roots* has come to occupy), the suggestion would be that a diaspora only becomes rhizomatic when it abandons attachment to a homeland. But in what does it then consist, and in any case, why should we assume that this is preferable—unless, of course, we have already decided that negative freedom is preferable to anamnestic solidarity?

The tentative suggestion therefore is that Deleuze and Guattari, in attempting to uproot the genealogical tree metaphor of (any) diasporic identity, unwittingly readmit an imperious and statist denial of the claims of any collective *name*. Paradoxically, even their own challenge to purist cultural genealogies has just been shown to be "rooted" at least partly in a particular diasporic tradition (as shown by the recourse to Weinreich's work, which grows out of the Bundist formulation of Jewish diasporism). The ability of this particular diaspora to "speak"—the possibility of a Jewish diasporic voice—is in turn tied largely to the technologies of anamnesia, inscription, and rediasporization mentioned earlier.

On the other hand, it is hardly surprising, even if distressing, that Deleuze and Guattari suppress Jewish difference *after 70 B.C.*[20] by totalizing a West (rooted) versus a ludicrously stereotypical East (rhizomatic) (18). Jews will never fit into such a dichotomy, which is one of the most important powers of the Jewish diaspora. Indeed, one of the critical factors stimulating the disruptive intervention of Jewish culture within the centuries-long effort to understand a certain "Europe" as "the West" with a primarily Greco-Roman heritage is the fact that the legal, ritual, and cultural interpretive tradition established precisely in "Asian" Babylonia achieved preeminence as an authoritative reference almost everywhere in the Jewish world (including, of course, among Afro-Asiatic Jews), effectively supplanting the "homeland" Palestinian interpretive tradition (for the effect of this on discourses of sexuality and gender, for example, see D. Boyarin 1993).

Diasporic identities—always chronotopically specific, resting on the simultaneous inputs of a specific tradition and interaction with autonomous, often more powerful others—give the lie to the specifically modern mode of nationalism. In the modern, territorial nation-state space is made the unchanging ground of identity, changing "Territory into Tradition" and "the People into One" (Bhabha 1994, 149). Yet this sense of "nation" is not particularly old in European thinking about groups in relation to territory. The medieval trading "nations" were actually diasporic, consisting of communities of traders from the same place outside their homelands:

> The effort that characterized the entire Middle Ages, of allowing disputes abroad to be adjudicated by countrymen of the participants and sentence to be passed in accordance with their native laws . . . entailed the necessity of setting up one of the eldest of the "nation" as judges, who were then charged with representing the common interests to the authorities, with surveillance over the houses and chapels of the nation, and with collecting the dues owed by the countrymen. (Friedrich Engels, cited in Nerlich 1987, 77)

Meanwhile, Denys Hay tells us that "[t]he original nations, into which the council [at Constance in 1417] was divided for deliberative purposes, were based on those found in the big arts faculties at universities, the practice of Paris being most influential" (1957, 77–78). The nation thus first exists as an extraterritorial, juridical, and commercial collective. How different is this from, for example, the structure of the Jewish community in ancient Alexandria, whose members had "a chief *(ethnarches),* their own tax inspector *(alabarches),* and, according to Strabo, formed a separate state unit *(politeia)*" (Dubnow 1931, 127)?

Yet the theory of the state continues to claim the nation as its own. Diasporas—or at least their "leaders," however the latter may come to enjoy that designation—may also indulge in unitarian rhetoric. The permanent slogan of the Federation of Jewish Philanthropies is quite blunt: "We [the Jewish people, that is] are one, in Israel and around the world." Of course this is a slogan about the need for solidarity versus a more powerful (and, implicitly, also monolithic!) "outside world," about the importance of hanging together in order to avoid hanging separately.[21] The notion that "in the group lies strength" might at first blush seem to echo an old Yiddish proverb: *kohol iz shtark,* which means "the [organized] community is strong." Historically, however, the saying *kohol iz shtark* bears an ominous connotation. It suggests the power exercised by the more powerful representatives of the corporate community—those responsible for the community's dealings with the authorities—over poorer and weaker members. This communal strength was often bitterly resented because of the impositions exacted against the weaker community members in order to meet the demands of the State, thereby maintaining simultaneously (and this entanglement is of critical importance) both the privileged position of the leadership and the often marginal existence of the community taken as a whole. The most dramatic form of this helpless oppressive power in the Russian empire is encapsulated in the figure of the dreaded *khapers,* Jewish kidnappers employed by communal officials to seize Jewish boys who were then sent to fulfill the twenty-five-year draftee quotas set by the Russian government.

This is "power," then, but power without freedom. This irony echoes the incisive point made by Barbara Kirshenblatt-Gimblett in response to Clifford when she states that even if Jewish diaspora is taken as normative, this use of the term "normative" actually refers to the situation of a group taken as the paradigmatic case of a number of *pathological* syndromes in social theory (Kirshenblatt-Gimblett 1994). Responding to Clifford's warning about "the risk of making Jewish experience once again the normative model" (Clifford 1994, 334), Kirshenblatt-Gimblett draws on the stance of insider retort: "this is not a site of privilege" (1994, 340). She is right: Jewish diaspora should not be glamorized to the point of theoretical envy; just because Jews have gotten so much attention as a diasporic people does not mean, of course, that they have enjoyed greater power or security in the everyday. Jewish diaspora is and is not privileged: it is sometimes recognized as the model, but, to the extent that organized Jewish strategies of security in the United States have focused on the desirability, feasibility, and appropriateness of assimilation, and to the extent that Jews see themselves and are seen as "white," Jewish self-constructions in the arena of ethnic politics further a displacement of Jewish studies from the emerging cultural studies apparatus of comparative diaspora, which in many instances appears to be an appropriately and effectively reinvigorated casting of affirmative action programs. Furthermore, to focus on the creative powers of diaspora within the institutional framework of academic Jewish studies is a risky business. Paradoxically, at a time when Israelocentrism is both rigidly enforced and increasingly questioned, even many Jewish academic scholars are liable to see a critical plea for the value and vitality of diaspora in Jewish life as betraying an unwonted Jewish capitulation to what the critical academy in general would like Jews to say about themselves, rather than what is truly in Jewish collective self-interest. Meanwhile the particular complications and resources that have enabled the Jewish diaspora have hardly begun to be articulated in the frame of comparative diaspora studies, and much of the critical potential of that emergent field will dissipate if the move to "deprivilege" *in the realm of theory* the dynamics of Jewish collective existence means that diaspora will be another aspect of cultural studies where Jews are marginalized from the multicultural matrix.

Tricksters, Martyrs, and Collaborators

*Diaspora and the Gendered
Politics of Resistance*

Tricksters, Martyrs, and Collaborators

Diaspora and the Gendered Politics of Resistance

Merneptah's epitaph for the Israelites was premature, for it was precisely the ability of the Jews to survive in a hostile imperial world that constituted their political genius.

—D. Biale, Power and Powerlessness in Jewish History

The genius of the Jewish people is diaspora.

—Sidney Boyarin

The Diaspora People as a Woman

Esther, Ya'el, and Judith save themselves and the Jewish people by seducing and deceiving a powerful male gentile. They are all highly valued within the Jewish hermeneutic tradition, and, to the best of our knowledge, never condemned for their deviousness in achieving victory over stronger male adversaries. We would like to suggest that the Jews identified themselves as a people with these heroines, and thus as female, with the appropriation of tactics of survival that belonged "by nature" to women. A nineteenth-century Danish theologian, Hans Lassen Martensen, saw a similar connection. He observed that "Women try to gain power through craft as well as dissimulation, intrigues, tricks, and lying . . . [and he] illustrated this corruption of female nature with reference to powerful women of ancient Israel and Judaism" (Briggs 1985, 236). For Jews, however, dissimulation, intrigues, tricks, and lying were valued when they served the purpose of survival, and the powerful women of ancient Israel who employed these tactics were valued as well.[1] It is no accident that Martensen chose this example, for it was a European topos that Jews used such "womanly" arts. Carl Jung represents a more refined (and somewhat sympathetic) version of this commonplace when he writes, "The Jews have this peculiarity in common with women; being physically weaker, they have to aim at the chinks in the armour of their adversary, and thanks to this technique which has been forced on them through the centuries, the Jews themselves are best protected where others are most vulnerable" (Jung 1970, 165).

In a recent essay Amy-Jill Levine has advanced our knowledge of the antecedents of rabbinic Judaism's femminized self-understanding (1992).[2] In the pre-rabbinic dystopic vision of the Book of Tobit, "In exile, dead bodies lie in the streets and those who inter them are punished; demons fall in love with women and kill their husbands; even righteousness is no guarantee of stability" (105).[3] The text, according to Levine, has three strategies in order to provide a "clear solid ground for self-definition." Of these three, the one that holds the most interest for our project is "a series of boundary-breaking events—eating, defecating, inseminating, interring," that function "to institute, transgress, and then reinforce distinctions."[4] Readers familiar with Bakhtin will immediately perceive that we are in the realm of the grotesque body, the permeable, quintessentially female (birth-giving, lactating) body, interacting and intersecting with the world and not closed in on itself, as the body of autochthony, the classical (male) body, would be. This body, of course, has both utopic and dystopic aspects. On the one hand, it is the vulnerable body, the body that is invaded, penetrated, and hurt. On the other hand, it is the fecund body, the body that interacts with the world and creates new life (Bakhtin 1984)—in short, a perfect representation of the dangers and the powers of diaspora. As Levine has remarked, "Woman is, in effect, in a perpetual diaspora; her location is never her own, but is contingent on that of her father, husband, or sons" (1992, 110). No wonder then, that the diasporic people imagine themselves as female. In Levine's reading—inspired by Mary Douglas—of Tobit's representations of the body as the corporate body of the Jews, only the negative side of this equation seems to be mobilized; the only products of the grotesque body are abjects (114). This parallels the point made by Briggs that within the anti-Semitic imaginary the "femaleness" of Jews is only a negative representation (1985, 256). For the Hellenistic Book of Tobit, diaspora is wholly deleterious, as expressed by Levine's statement that "As a woman, as unaware, as unable to interact, as impeded from conceiving, Sarah cannot represent the covenant community. Instead, unless she is redeemed by the community's pure, male representatives, Sarah represents what could be its fate in the diaspora: ignorant, childless, and in the undesired embrace of idolatry represented by the demon" (1992, 112).

The gendered representation of the social body of Israel shifts between the Judaism represented by the Book of Tobit and that of the Rabbis of late antiquity. For the Hellenistic-Jewish novella, only a male figure can represent Israel (Levine 1992, 113); the Rabbis can conceive of themselves, and of the people, as female. We might conceive of this as a move from a Douglassian world within which the primary concern is the reestablishing of the chaotic and threatened borders of purity to a Bakhtinian one in which it is precisely the breaching of borders of the social/individual body that produces life; from one in which diaspora and femminization[5] of the social body are seen only as a threat to one in which they are celebrated (however warily) for their ethical and creative possibilities.[6]

Tobit is dreaming of an immediate end to diaspora; for the Rabbis it has become the condition of their lives as Jews. For the Rabbis, especially the Babylonian ones, the condition of diaspora held spiritual promise as well as danger, purity in the midst of impurity. To be sure, for the Rabbis as well, "[the woman's] identity only assumes meaning when she becomes a wife," but wifehood had very positive significance. Israel, after all, was God's wife. This did not cash out as a better life for human wives. Thus, all of their more positive sense of sexuality and wifehood did not necessarily change the fact that, as Levine so acutely concludes, "By constraining women's roles, by using women as tokens of exchange to preserve kinship and economic ties, by depicting them as the cause as well as the locus of despair, and by removing them from direct contact with heaven, the Jewish male [of the Book of Tobit] has brought order to his diaspora existence. In captivity, he can assert his freedom and his self-identity by depicting the other as in captivity to him" (117). This same critique, valid as well for the Rabbis, must be kept in mind constantly. We can go on to explore the ways that Jewish maleness was, nevertheless, a form of resistance to Roman phallic masculinity.

Kaja Silverman's recent account of the "dominant fiction" and its relation to history seems to us an important step forward. This dominant fiction of which she speaks is constituted by the myth of the equation of the penis to the phallus, that is, by a narrative that defines maleness through ascribing to the male an "unimpaired bodily 'envelope' . . . fiercely protective of its coherence" (1992, 61). The penis become phallus becomes then the very symbol of power and privilege as well as of completeness, coherence, univocity. And thus Silverman concludes, "Conventional masculinity can best be understood as the denial of castration, and hence as a refusal to acknowledge the defining limits of subjectivity. The category of 'femininity' is to a very large degree the result" (46).

Silverman refers to this constellation as "the dominant fiction." Her very use of the term "fiction," and its association with the political power implied by "dominant" as well, suggests strongly a particular historical, cultural construct. This would pose the possibility of other cultures having other dominant fictions, other narratives of how male is symbolically related to female. However, at other points in Silverman's discourse she seems rather to accept than contest a certain psychoanalytic version that would read this narrative not as the dominant fiction of a particular cultural formation but rather as the normal, structuring organization of the human psyche, always and everywhere, except when (temporarily) ruptured by particular "historical" circumstances. Thus at one point she writes:

> By "historical trauma" we mean a historically precipitated but psychoanalytically specific disruption, with ramifications extending far beyond the individual psyche. To state the case more precisely, we mean any historical event, whether socially engineered or of natural occurrence, which brings a large group of male subjects into such an intimate relation with lack that they are at least for the moment unable to sustain an imaginary relation with the phallus, and so withdraw their belief from the dominant fiction. Suddenly the latter is radically de-realized, and the social formation finds itself without a mechanism for achieving consensus. (1992, 55)

This formulation clearly portrays the dominant fiction not only as dominant but as normal, allowing itself to be interrupted only under the pressure of extreme and even violent circumstance, such as war, i.e., that sort of "historical event . . . that brings a large group of male subjects into such an intimate relation with lack that they are *at least for the moment* unable to sustain an imaginary relation with the phallus" (emphasis obviously added). In other words, the default situation is one in which male subjects are so out of touch with lack, so protected against their own "castration," that they can imagine that the penis is identical to the phallus and thus project all lack onto female subjects. This ordinary situation, however, by being contrasted to history, is itself projected as being beyond history or above and outside of history and thus, as in Lacan (and Freud) as being beyond and outside of a particular cultural formation. This argument is only strengthened by the apparent implication of Silverman's text that the social formation (any social formation?) can only achieve consensus, i.e., maintain hegemony and continue to exist through *this* particular dominant fiction, that is, the one that "forgets" that all humans are "castrated."

It seems to us that the problems that are raised by Silverman's project for itself are occasioned precisely by the commitment to a Lacanian phallus that is not the penis. Indeed, for Lacan it is only the *equation* of the phallus with the penis that would lead to "an unproblematic assertion of male privilege." Such an equation, however, is always, necessarily, and paradoxically implied by the very separation/idealization of the phallus that European culture—including Lacan—promotes.[7] Silverman herself has apparently realized this very point, for she writes in an essay after her book, "Recent theory has benefited enormously from Lacan's distinction between the penis and the phallus. We have learned from that distinction that the male sexual organ can never be equivalent to the values designated by the phallus, and that consequently all subjects might be said to be castrated. However, the metaphorics of veiling and unveiling deployed by Lacan . . . suggest that it may not always be politically productive to differentiate sharply between penis and phallus" (1992, 89). This is a step forward, but we would argue that differentiation between penis and phallus, i.e., the very myth of the phallus, is *never* politically productive. The issue is not whether we differentiate sharply or fuzzily but whether we posit a phallus at all. It is the very transcendent immateriality of the phallus, and thus its separation from the penis, that constitutes its ability to project masculinity as the universal—as the Logos—and by doing so significantly enables both male and imperial projects of domination. A strong case can be made that this particular mode of idealization of the male body was instrumental, if not necessary, in the erection—pun intended—of empires, whether Roman or modern.

Precisely because the penis is *not* the phallus but signifies the phallus, any theory of subjectivity that bases itself on the phallus and castration will always be an instrument in the service of the dominant fiction, the European cultural myth of masculinity. In this sense our position here is almost the exact opposite of that of Jane Gallop who argues that the inability to keep phallus and penis separate is a "symptom of the impossibility, at this moment in our history, to think a masculine that is not phallic, a masculine that can couple with a feminine," and further that "this double-bind combination of necessity and impossibility produces the endless repetition of failed efforts to clearly distinguish phallus and penis" (1988, 127). Gallop ends her meditation still longing for a phallus that could be separated from the penis, or rather a penis that is separated from the transcendent phallus (131). We maintain that the phallus itself, and its necessary inseparability from the penis for deep historical and linguistic reasons,[8] is one of the factors that make it difficult (not impossible, in our view) to refigure masculinity in our culture and in this time.[9] Nancy K. Miller seems very much on point here when she doubts that "nondiscursive practices will respond correctly to the correct theory of discursive practice" and worries that "glossing 'woman' as an archaic signifier glosses over the *referential* suffering of women" (1990, 114) . The same, mutatis mutandis, applies to the nonreferentiality of the phallus. It may escape gravity; it will not escape the penis (Bernheimer 1992).

In addition to war, Silverman describes certain Christian formations of masculinity as being marginal to male subjectivity, putting maleness as masculinity into question through various extreme corporeal behaviors, such as martyrdom or extreme ascetic practice (192). She also recognizes a category of disempowered males whose phallic identification is at risk:

"Oppression experienced in relation to class, race, ethnicity, age, and other ideologically determined 'handicaps' may also pose major obstacles in the way of a phallic identification, or may expose masculinity as a masquerade" (47). The very language chosen here, however, in spite of the scare quotes, indicates the position taken. These male subjectivities, as well as the male victims of war and gay men, are inscribed by Silverman as marginal to the ordinary, the timeless, the normal form of male subjectivity, in spite of the explicit challenge to that kind of male subjectivity that Silverman wishes to urge. Moreover, this account renders problematic Silverman's own political desire to promote a different practice or performance of male subjectivity.

Rather than seeing the breakdown of the phallic imaginary as a product of trauma, as does Kaja Silverman, earliest Christian (until Constantine) and Jewish texts present a culture of men who are resisting, renouncing, and disowning the phallus. Compare the view of Aviva Cantor who writes, "It was primarily because survival during the national emergency of Exile required the community to be a safe haven that male violence had to be eliminated" (1995, 4–5). While we agree that there was a significant diminution (if not "elimination") of male violence, our positions are nearly diametrically opposed as to the interpretation of the cause and effect relations of that process. Cantor (15–16) explicitly argues against the "Diasporist" position that we inhabit. It follows that our positions on the causal links between neo-machismo among Jews and Zionism are reversed. Where Cantor sees the machismo as an effect of a "combination of circumstances, including the ongoing state of siege," we see such "recrudescence of traditional [i.e., European] normative patriarchal roles" (6) as the very goal of Herzlian-Nordovian Zionism. In general, we find her functional explanations unconvincing: for example, it seems highly implausible to assume that the ideology of chivalry did not develop in Jewish societies because Jewish men were unable to defend "their" women (88). This formulation assumes the naturalness of the male role as protector, whereas it is precisely that discourse of natural gender roles that we believe Jewish culture helps dislocate. For this reason, we find the following statement almost invidious: "While the sages condemned David's wars, later scholars suggested that the king had waged them to prevent the capture and rape of Jewish women. This points to a yearning on the part of Jewish men to prevent such rapes. The yearning, however, was not acknowledged because it would have reinforced the men's anxiety about their powerlessness in the Exile and their shame about not fulfilling the classic role that defines masculinity under patriarchy: protecting and defending 'their' women. These feelings were kept at bay by the defense mechanism of denial—not of the prevalence and threat of rape but of the men's responsibility to prevent it" (89). This formulation assumes either a natural status for that "classic role that defines masculinity" or an undertheorized total internalization of the dominant fiction by Jewish men. Such essentialization of the male role is typical of Zionist ideology (90)—and indeed almost constitutive thereof (D. Boyarin 2000).[10]

This is entirely clear with respect to the early Christians. Since many of them were men of power and status in their pre-Christian lives, it is hard to argue that it was trauma that dislodged the dominant fiction for them. Ambrose was a provincial governor before his conversion, so, for him, becoming Christian was truly a renunciation of the phallus, as it was for his compatriot, Prudentius, and many others at the time. Their status in the church, while it had many attributes of power, had to be configured differently from their former status (Burrus 1994). If anything, it was their resistance to the dominant fiction that brought trauma upon them and not the opposite. It is clear that the "phallus" was renounced and resisted by them as a particular cultural product, one belonging to a culture they had rejected. The peculiar promise of the Jewish text, on the other hand, seems to be in its premise that such a renunciation does not imply an exit from male sexuality entirely. It was the condition of not being imperial, of being diasporic, that presents this possibility to the Rabbis, a possibility not of a temporary disruption but of demystifying "the phallus" for what it is, a violent and destructive ideological construct. Instead of reading this alternative mode of constructing maleness as anomalous, thus accepting the terms of the dominant fiction as reality, we offer an antithetical reading of Jewish history, one in which the absence of the phallus is a positive product of cultural history and not a signifier of disease. Rather than seeing these responses as evidence of a pathology, we would suggest that in their political and cultural opposition to the tyranny of the Roman Empire, both Rabbis and early Christians developed positively marked images of femminized men, thus marking the site of a cultural crisis for the Roman Empire that, it could be argued, led eventually to its breakdown.

In the text that we will be reading first, the intimate connections among sexuality, politics, and gender are directly thematized. Hundreds of years later than the Book of Tobit, the rabbinic texts of the Babylonian Talmud also use the body as a symbol for the diasporic people. Yet rabbinic fantasies about Rabbis and Romans evoke much more complex and nuanced ways of considering the gendered social body of the Jewish people in diaspora. A "woman" is now not only she whose purity is threatened, but also she who has powers and potentialities for survival. In the next section of this analysis, we will contrast two Jewish paradigms of resistance to Roman domination, the first from Josephus (as selectively incorporated into modern Jewish and especially Zionist collective memory), and the second from the classic of rabbinic culture, the Babylonian Talmud (as canonized in the traditional memory of Diaspora Jews).

Masada or Yavneh?

"Be as quiet as water and lower than the grass."

—*Russian rabbi, in response to Kishinev pogrom of 1903*

"Be obscure and live!"
— *Babylonian Talmud Sanhedrin*

The fable of Masada is so familiar by now that it is almost cliché. The Jews have fought bravely for three years,[11] the end is near, and hope for victory is gone. Rather than submit to slavery, in the night the adult male Jews kill all their women and children and then the male Jews are killed by the swords of their fellows. The last alive kill themselves. The events at Masada, or better the Masada myth (Ben-Yehuda 1995), have become, (in)famously, paradigmatic for a certain modern Jewish consciousness. But it was not always so. Indeed, when the Jewish settlement of Palestine was founded in modern times, no one knew how to spell the name Masada in Hebrew, so an early kibbutz (founded 1937) that took the name used the Greek version. A recent critic notes that the Josephus text was preserved only by Christians and adds: "The story of the fall of Masada thus did not vanish from the records of Jewish history, but it disappeared from the Jews' collective memory" (Zerubavel 1994, 75).[12] The Masada myth has everything to do, we will argue, with manliness. It is accordingly very important in understanding the gendered politics of rabbinic Judaism to gain some insight into the rejection of Masada as a model for Jewish behavior, indeed as even a memory.

While scholars have long realized, of course, that the leader El'azar's speech reported by Josephus is a historiographical fiction, modeled on Roman exemplars and topoi (Vidal-Naquet 1983), they have not emphasized enough how totally the situation and events, the very narrative, and even more to the point, its values are historically suspect (Zerubavel 1995, 197).[13] An appropriate comparison for the suicide rather than surrender might be the behavior of Cato the Younger, who fell on his sword rather than be pardoned by Caesar, thus becoming his dependent.[14] We are appalled to hear Lucan's Vulteius, addressing his troops on the eve of their mass and mutual suicide, declare that their honor would be greater if their children and old folks were there to die with them. ("In not holding us captive together with our old folks and children, envious Fortune has subtracted much from our honor" [abscidit nostrae multum fors invida laudi, / quod non cum senibus capti natisque tenemur] [Bellum civile 4.503–4] [Barton 1994]). The Roman audience could read the agonizing act at Masada through their own tradition. They had, after all, refused to ransom their prisoners of war from Hannibal after the battle of Cannae (in which they had lost at least fifty thousand men). And so the Romans might have understood that no one could break the spirit of the Jews so long as a Jewish mother was willing to see her children tortured to death rather than submit to the tyrant Antiochus (2 and 4 Maccabees). Masada would be what Cannae was for the Romans: the disaster that galvanized the Jewish spirit—the diamond spirit produced under the overwhelming pressure of despair. A Roman reading Josephus's account might have thought that the Jews at Masada had one-upped Lucan's Vulteius and his doomed and devoted soldiers: they had their children and old folks there to die with them. The "Romanness" of the narrative ought indeed to make us very wary of the historicity of the events reported only by Josephus.[15] His defenders of Masada, the Sicarii (dagger men), are Jews who escaped the domination of Rome by turning themselves into real Roman men in dying rather than submitting. The Romans came finally to respect them, says Josephus, owing to their contempt for death, but the Rabbis, in turn, despised them. Nor is this terribly surprising. As Nachman Ben-Yehuda emphasizes, the Sicarii, according to Josephus, were assassins driven out of Jerusalem by Jews; they subsisted on Masada by raiding Jewish villages and perpetrated a terrible massacre of seven hundred Jewish women and children at Ein Gedi (9).

What is more surprising is that the Zionist propaganda machine turned these thugs into its greatest heroes.[16] The Israeli general and archeologist, excavator and producer of

Masada,[17] Yigael Yadin, was thoroughly moved by what he took as Josephus's realistic account:

> No one could have matched [Josephus's] gripping description of what took place on the summit of Masada on that fateful night in the spring of 73 A.D. Whatever the reasons, whether the pangs of conscience or some other cause we cannot know, the fact is that his account is so detailed and reads so faithfully, and his report of the words uttered by Elazar ben Yair is so compelling, that it seems evident that he had been genuinely overwhelmed by the record of heroism on the part of the people he had forsaken. (1966, 15)

We would argue that far from being a conscience-ridden return to and valorization of "his" people,[18] the account of the honorable suicide to avoid surrender at Masada was another step in Josephus's self-Romanization. It was, accordingly, a further betrayal (or, alternatively, another step in the self-justification of his betrayal). Similarly, the adoption of this myth by Yadin was a maneuver in the modern transformation of "sheep-like effeminate" Jews into real Israeli men.[19] For evidence of how thoroughly the "Roman" ethos was internalized in modern Zionist culture, the following account by Yael Zerubavel will suffice: "A member of a [Palestinian Jewish Zionist] youth movement expressed his and his friends' reluctance to participate in the days of mourning in solidarity with European Jewry [while the genocide was taking place!], claiming that instead his movement's gathering at Masada was a sufficient expression of their solidarity with those Jews who did not choose servitude." Zerubavel notes that even during the 1960s in Israel, "the partisans and the Ghetto fighters" were honored "as 'Zionist' or 'Hebrew Youth,'" but the Israeli official discourse referred to "the other Holocaust victims as Jews" (1995, 80). In contrast to earlier Passover Haggadah, in which the wicked son was nearly always some sort of soldier or military figure, in the Haggadah published in the year of Israeli independence by the Haggana Shock

Troops, the "heroes" are respectively a ghetto fighter, portrayed as a Hasid with a machine gun—ignoring, of course,
the fact that the rebels of the Warsaw ghetto were thoroughly
secular—and an Israeli guerilla.

The exemplary rabbinic moment of truth was entirely
opposite to Masada.[20] Here is the tale as it is told in the Babylonian Talmud, Gittin 56a-b (following the text in Ms. Vati-
can 140), in which the opposition to Masada's heroes, here
referred to as "hooligans" is articulated:

> Father of Lies,[21] the leader of the hooligans in Jerusalem, was
> the nephew of Rabbi Yoḥanan ben Zakkai. He [Yoḥanan] sent
> to him [Father of Lies]: "Come to me in secret!" He came. He
> [Yoḥanan] said: "How long will you continue to do thus [re-
> fuse to make peace, Rashi] and kill everyone with hunger?"
> He [Father of Lies] said: "And what can I do? If I say any-
> thing to them [my (erstwhile) comrades, the hooligans], they
> will kill me!" He [Yoḥanan] said: "If you see a solution for
> me, I will go out. Perhaps there will be some measure of salva-
> tion." He [Father of Lies] said: "Proclaim yourself sick, and
> everyone will come to ask about you. Then take something
> stinking to place next to you and they will say that you have
> died. Then have your students [carry the bier], for they [the
> hooligans] know that the live are lighter than the dead."
>
> He did so. Rabbi Eliᶜezer on one side and Rabbi Yehoshuᶜa
> on the other went in [to carry the bier]. When they arrived at
> the door, they [the hooligans] wanted to pierce him. They [the
> students] said: "The Romans will say that you have pierced
> your rabbi." They wished to push him. They said: "They will
> say that you pushed your rabbi."
>
> They opened the gate.
>
> When they arrived there [at the Roman encampment]. He
> [Yoḥanan] said: "Peace be upon you, O king!" He [Vespasian]
> said: "You are now liable to be put to death twice. First of all,
> I am not king [and you called me king], and second, if indeed
> I am king, why did you not come to me until now?"

He [Yoḥanan] said: "As for what you said that you are not king; indeed, you are a king";[22] for were he not a king, Jerusalem would not have been given over into his hands, as it says, "The Lebanon[23] will fall before the mighty" [Isaiah 10:34], and there is no mighty other than a king; as it says, "His mighty one will be from him; [his ruler] will arise from his midst" [Jeremiah 30:21].

And as for what you said that if you are king, why have I not come until now; the hooligans that are here did not let me."

He [Vespasian] said to him: "If there is a barrel of honey and a snake is wrapped around it, would you not break the barrel, in order to get rid of the dragon?" [i.e., should you not have broken down the walls in order to destroy the hooligans, Rashi].

He [Yoḥanan] was silent.

Rabbi Akiva applied to him [Vespasian] the verse: "He overturns the wise and confuses their judgment" [Isaiah 44:25]; "He should have said, 'We would take a tongs, remove the dragon, kill it, and leave the barrel sound'" [i.e., we hoped to be able to defeat and kill the hooligans, make peace with you, and leave Jerusalem intact].

By and by, there came a messenger from the king saying: "Arise, for the king is dead, and the leaders of Rome [the Senate] have appointed you king!" . . .

He [Vespasian] said: "Ask of me something, and I will give it to you."

He [Yoḥanan] said: "Give me Yavne and its sages, and the dynasty of Rabban Gamliel, and doctors to cure Rabbi Ẓadoq [who had been fasting in order to save Jerusalem]."

Given the almost identical situation and the exactly opposite response, it would not be going too far to speculate that here we have the only possible allusion to Masada that there is in rabbinic literature—and that, of course, only via a suppression. The Rabbis of our Talmudic text reveal their stance vis-à-vis the Sicarii—the defenders of Masada who are also those who, in Jerusalem, are refusing any peace treaty with Rome—by dubbing them "hooligans." The protagonists of Josephus's narrative are called "hooligans" and seen as more of an enemy than Rome itself and its Emperor Vespasian. Whether or not, however, this is an actual reference to the Masada narrative, the almost exact reversal of values that it encodes is highly significant. This narrative is the Babylonian founding myth of the rabbinic movement, for Rabbi Yoḥanan ben Zakkai and his students—Yavne and its sages—are the mythical foundation of all of rabbinic literature.[24]

Thus we see at the foundation of the rabbinic value system the obverse of the "manly" Roman values in the Masada foundation myth of Jewish heroism. Rabbi Yoḥanan's story makes nearly explicit allusion to Josephus, since according to the latter, it was he who announced to Vespasian that he had become emperor. This helps to establish an intertextual connection between the texts and promotes contrast of their values. The Babylonian Talmud's Rabbi Yoḥanan prefers life and the possibility to serve God through the study of Torah over everything else. He is willing to abase himself, pretend to be dead—a virtual parody of the Masada suicide?—make peace with the Romans over/against the Jewish zealots, even to sacrifice Jerusalem, in order that Jewish life and Torah might continue. Where the Josephan zealots proved themselves "real men" by preferring death at their own hands to slavery, the Rabbis prefer slavery to death.

There is an issue that must be clarified here, lest we be misunderstood. None of the rabbis were pacifists, nor did they advocate "turning the other cheek."[25] When the Rabbis had to choose to preserve life through violence or to die, the choice was clear: choose life. The options we are discussing are rather death with "honor" versus "shameful" death, or, even more sharply, versus life as a slave. We contend that the choice of "death with (so-called) honor"—as in the Zionist appropriations of the Warsaw Ghetto revolt, harking back to the Masada ideal—represents a cultural capitulation that does not honor Jewish difference, while the choice to live however one can and continue to create as Jews is resistance. And thus it remains. When the rabbi quoted earlier advocated remaining "as quiet as water and lower than the grass," he was not promoting suicide but a resistant strategy for remaining alive and continuing as Jews. The socialist co-commander of the Warsaw Revolt, the anti-Zionist Marek Edelman, who remains in Poland as a diaspora Jewish (Yiddish) nationalist and member of Solidarity, saw this very clearly: "This was a revolt? The whole point was not to let them slaughter you when your turn came. The whole point was to choose your method of dying. All of humanity had already agreed that dying with a weapon in the hand is more beautiful than without a weapon. *So we surrendered to that consensus*" (Zertal 1994). The notion that dying with a weapon is more beautiful and honorable than dying without one is a surrender of Jewish difference to a "universal," masculinist consensus.[26] Modern Jewish culture (not only Zionist) has assimilated the macho male ethos of Western civilization. The result is the creation of the "Muscle Jew" (Nordau 1980), which divorces Jewish men from their emphasis on study, prayer, and gentleness. Ironically, in an effort to counter the anti-Semitic image of the so-called Jewish wimp, Jewish men have abetted a process of internal colonization of Jewish culture by mainstream Christian culture and have adopted the anti-Semite's aggressive heterosexuality.

As Carlin Barton has remarked: "Seneca despises the caged, mutilated and degraded King Telesphorus of Rhodes for clinging to life at the price of his honor (*Epistulae* 70.6–7; cf. *De ira* 3.17.3–4), and brands his famous aphorism, 'Where there's life there's hope,' as 'effeminatissima'" (1993, 30). "Where there's life there's hope," or "Where there's life there's Torah," could practically be the motto of the rabbinic movement from Rabbi Yoḥanan ben Zakkai onward, and it was, therefore, "effeminatissima." Zionist ideology completely absorbed this

"Roman" value system. Thus "a prominent Palestinian Zionist leader, Yitzhak Gruenbaum, stated that 'the trouble of the Diaspora Jews is that they preferred the life of a "beaten dog" over dignified death.' He continued by urging to prepare for a last stand that would allow the settlers at least to leave behind 'a Masada legend'" (Zerubavel 1995, 73). In contrast to the Zionists, Schopenhauer seems certainly to have understood something bona fide about Judaic culture in his insistence that it is characterized by an "optimistic" will to live, which he, of course, despises, as he despises everything "effeminate" (Le Rider 1995, 27–28).

The Ways of Peace: Understanding a Hidden Transcript

Another text, this time from the Palestinian Talmud,[27] explicitly recommends appeasement (not, of course, the same thing as collaboration) as the appropriate response to oppressive power. Appeasement is the expression of a will to live that masculinist romance culture would consider *effeminatissima*.

> How does Rabbi Ḥiyya the Great explain the verse: "You shall buy food from them for money and eat"?—If you feed him, you have bought and broken him, for if he is harsh with you, buy/break him with food, and if [that does] not [work], then defeat him with money.
>
> They say: That is how Rabbi Yonatan behaved. When he saw a powerful personage come into his city, he used to send him expensive things. What did he think? If he comes to judge an orphan or a widow, we will find him propitious towards them. (Yerushalmi Shabbat 1:3, 3c)

Rabbi Ḥiyya develops a whole political philosophy of Jewish-gentile interaction—actually of Jewish-*Roman* interaction—from this verse. His reading is justified by the fact that the verse actually does refer to the proper behavior of Israel toward Esau, the eponymous ancestor of Rome in rabbinic Jewish lore. The Bible explicitly says not to provoke them.[28] An alternative to provoking them is also offered by the verse, which

Rabbi Ḥiyya understands in a way that takes it out of its immediate biblical historical context and gives it new cultural
power. He reads it as a suggestion to use gifts to turn the
rulers' hearts favorably to their Jewish subjects. This is derived from the verse by typically clever midrashic punning, in
addition to the mobilization of the foundational intertext: the
story of the original Jacob and Esau. Without forcing the lexi-
con and with only relatively modest stretching of the syntax—
well within the bounds of midrashic practice—the phrase
"buy food from them" can also be read as "break them," i.e.,
defeat them, since the word "buy" and the word "break" are
homonyms. The verse is thus read as: "With food, buy them,
and [if that doesn't work] break [suborn] them with money
[baksheesh]." This is an obvious allusion to the situation
within which the weak, "feminine" Jacob bought the favor of
the "virile," dominant Esau by giving him food. Baksheesh itself becomes institutionalized as a discursive practice of opposition to oppression. At additional points in this discussion,
we will be observing how various "dishonest" practices, de-
ceptions, are valorized by rabbinic and other colonized peoples
in direct opposition to the "manly" arts of violent resistance.[29]
As an Indian untouchable phrased it: "We must also tactfully
disguise and hide, as necessary, our true aims and intentions
from our social adversaries. To recommend it is not to en-
courage falsehood but only to be tactical in order to survive"
(Scott 1990, 33).

The Seductions of Jesus: Rabbi Eliʿezer and the Christian

A Talmudic narrative explicitly thematizes the virtue of the
trickster and his sharp practices in a situation of colonial
domination:[30]

> When Rabbi Eliʿezer was arrested [by the Romans] for sectari-
> anism [Christianity], they took him up to the place of judg-
> ment *[gradus]*.[31] The judge *[hegemon]*[32] said to him: "An
> elder such as you, has dealing with these foolish things?" He

[Eli'ezer] said: "I have trust in the J/judge." The judge thought that he was speaking about him, but he was speaking about his Father in heaven. He [the judge] said: "Since you have declared your faith in me, you are free *[dimus]*." When he came to his house, his disciples came to comfort him, but he was inconsolable. Rabbi Akiva said to him: "Allow me to say to you one of the things that you have taught me" [an honorific euphemism for the student teaching the teacher]. He said to him: "Say!" He said to him: "Rabbi, perhaps you heard some matter of sectarianism, and it gave you pleasure, and because of that you were arrested for sectarianism." He said: "By heaven, you have reminded me. Once I was walking in the upper market of Sephorris, and one of the disciples of Jesus the Nazarene,[33] a man by the name of Jacob of Kefar Sekania, met up with me. He said to me, 'It is written in your Torah: "Do not bring the wages of a prostitute or the proceeds of a dog" [to the house of your Lord] (Deut. 23:19). What about using them to build a latrine for the High Priest?' And I said nothing to him. And he told me that thus had taught Jesus his teacher: 'It was gathered from the wages of a prostitute, and to the wages of a prostitute it will return [Micah 1:7]—it comes from a place of filth, and to a place of filth it will return' [i.e., for building a latrine one may use the proceeds of a prostitute], and the matter gave me pleasure, and for that I was arrested for sectarianism, since I had violated that which is written: *Keep her ways far away from you!*" [Proverbs 5:8]. (Babylonian Talmud, Avoda Zara 16b)

This complex little text compresses within its almost humorous form several weighty matters of rabbinic culture and ideology. One of the matters that most concerns us here is the political function of the double entendre (Scott 1990, 153–54). This story exemplifies an almost literal thematization of the public transcript/hidden transcript typology as analyzed extensively by Scott. Dominated people, according to him, "make use of disguise, deception, and indirection while maintaining an outward impression, in power-laden situations, of willing, even enthusiastic consent" (1990, 17). Our Talmudic narrative seems designed to illustrate the hypothesis, for the narrative elegantly encapsulates the public and hidden transcripts into one ambiguous linguistic utterance. The text, however, has a theological dimension as well.

The basic theological question addressed is theodicy, a question that returns over and over in rabbinic literature: why has God punished the apparently righteous? As we shall see, this is one of the major subthemes of the entire text-sequence that we shall be following in this chapter. The basic rabbinic theological thought that answers this question is that somehow God's punishments fit the crimes—"measure for measure" in rabbinic parlance. When Rabbi Eliʿezer says in this text, "I have trust in the Judge," he fools the Roman *hegemon,* but not himself. He assumes that there cannot be any punishment without a crime and that the Divine Judge has found him wanting. The Roman judge is, in a sense, only an unwitting avatar of God's judgment on earth. The acceptance of the judgment is indeed what releases Rabbi Eliʿezer. This point will be returned to explicitly in a later episode of the legend cycle as well. In the context of the text that we are discussing here, this momentous theological issue is linked with other questions that the rabbis ask about themselves and their place in the world. This opening story sets all the themes that will be developed throughout the text: sex, heresy, and the threat of violence—in their own language: incest, idol worship, and spilling of blood. We will hardly be surprised to find gender prominently thematized in this context as well.

The strongest clue to this connection is the arbitrariness of the particular halakic discussion between the rabbi and the Christian, for there is no special reason why it would be this specific issue that a disciple of Jesus would raise with a Pharisee. The choice of an interlocution having to do with prostitution and the Temple must be laid at the door of the Talmudic "author" of this legend, and its significance sought

within the context of Jewish culture in general and this Talmudic passage specifically. We would suggest that the text is
here adumbrating a theme that will become more and more
explicit and insistent as the text continues, one that associates
prostitution both with heresy and with collaboration with
Roman power. This association will provide important links,
as we will see, to diaporic consciousness as well.

The connection would seem to be—beyond simple misogyny
that will associate anything negative with female sexuality—
that which is powerfully seductive, almost irresistible, but extremely dangerous at the same time. This association is thematized within the text through a powerful analogy between the
substance of the discourse of the "Christian" and the outcome
of enjoying that very discourse. The Christian proposes a le-
nient reading of the verse that prohibits the taking of the earnings of a prostitute to the Temple, namely, that although such
earnings are forbidden for holy purposes, for mundane—and
even lowly—purposes like the building of a toilet for the High
Priest, they are permitted. A fairly typical midrashic justification for this conclusion is proposed by the Christian as well.
Rabbi Eliʿezer "enjoys" this utterance, perhaps, for two reasons. First of all, there is the sheer intellectual pleasure of a
clever midrashic reading, one that, we emphasize, is in method
identical to "kosher" midrash, and second, the result of this
midrash would be increased funding for the Temple. The rabbi
is, however, punished for this enjoyment by the humiliation and
fright of being arrested by the Romans for being a Christian,
which he just barely escapes. The analogy seems clear: just as
one may not take the hire of a prostitute for any purpose connected with holiness, so one may not take the "Torah" of a
heretic for any purpose connected with holiness. Although the
substance of the words of Torah seem identical—just as the
money itself is identical—the source in "impurity" renders
them unfit for holiness and renders their acceptance punish-
able. Sectarianism is homologous with prostitution. Moreover, the seductiveness of the heretical interpretation matches

formally what its content encodes as well, for there also the
temptation is to use for holy purposes that which originates in
impurity, the harlot's wage. When Rabbi Eliᶜezer indicts himself for having violated the precept to "Keep her ways far
away from you!" both of these moments are comprehended.
In these stories, sexual temptation is the conflation of a variety
of different cultural tensions. Although the story is set (and
perhaps originally told) in the context of a world in which
both Jews and Christians (and Christians even more than
Jews) were together being persecuted by Romans, by the time
it becomes embedded within the Talmudic text, Christianity
has become Rome. At this point, resistance to Christianity becomes transformed into resistance to the domination of the
central power and thus the main topos for the production of
diasporic consciousness.

In the next section of the text that we will treat here, two
paradigmatic stories of response to Roman tyranny are presented with directly opposing ideologies. One will be an indirect echo of the story of Rabbi Eliᶜezer that we have encountered earlier, in which the potential martyr escapes through a
kind of tricksterism, while in the other, we have the model of
the defiant martyr par excellence. The two figures are actually
pitted against each other in the same story, thus thematizing
more directly the question of appropriate modes of resistance
within the diasporic situation. The story of Rabbi Eliᶜezer
that appeared in the beginning of the text provided only one
option, but now the options are multiplied and confronted in
the form of dialogue between the two rabbinic protagonists.

Although there is no direct resolution in the text of the
contention between "masculine" defiance and "feminine"
avoidance, and it would be foolhardy and reductive to produce one, we shall try, nevertheless, to show that in this text
deceptiveness and conniving are an honored alternative to defiance. We are not arguing that this text opposes martyrdom
tout court—martyrdom was too prestigious a cultural practice for that. Certainly this text questions the presumption

that defiance leading to glorified death is the only possible response to oppression. Finally, however, the text seems to say more about the impossibility of resistance than about its possibilities. The story opens:

> Our Rabbis have taught: When Rabbi El‘azar the son of Perata and Rabbi Ḥanina the son of Teradyon were arrested for sectarianism, Rabbi El‘azar the son of Perata said to Rabbi Ḥanina the son of Teradyon: "Happy art thou who has been arrested for only one thing. Woe unto me who has been arrested for five things." Rabbi Ḥanina the son of Teradyon said to him: "Happy art thou who has been arrested for five things and will be rescued. Woe unto me who has been arrested for one thing and will not be saved, for you busied yourself with Torah and with good deeds, while I only busied myself with Torah."—This is in accord with the view of Rav Huna who said that anyone who busies himself with Torah alone is as if he had no God. (Avoda Zarah 17)

As in the case of Rabbi Eli‘ezer with which the whole cycle opened, here also the Rabbis are very concerned to justify God's punishment of apparently righteous men via their arrest by the Roman authorities. This, in addition to its "universal" theological aspects, has particular resonance as part of the project of the production of a diaspora Judaism, since the form of cultural particularity within the dominant structure is being adumbrated as well. The notion that the oppressive empire is God's whip raises the question of resistance to a high theological pitch while reinstating a rather simple theodicy. The Rabbis, like Job's friends, cannot stand the thought of a God who punishes without cause.[34] In order, however, to preserve the sense of Rabbi Ḥanina's blamelessness and also to justify God's actions toward him, the Talmud cites a text that indicates that once he was holding two types of public moneys and he confused them and thus distributed the money intended for one purpose to the poor by mistake. For that lack of care in the administration of public money, he was arrested and martyred, and, moreover, it is this carelessness that justifies the judgment put in his own mouth that he had not engaged in good deeds![35]

The text goes on with the details of the trials of the two prisoners:

> They brought Rabbi El‛azar the son of Perata. They asked him: "Why did you teach and why did you steal?" He answered them: "If book, no sword and if sword, no book! Since one must be absent, the other must as well."

Rabbi El‛azar the son of Perata uses his wits to get himself out of trouble. He declares that there is a self-contradiction in the charges that they are accusing him of, for one cannot be both a scholar and a thief. Since, he says, the two accusations contradict each other, they cancel each other out. In effect, the rabbi is saying: Either you are accusing me of acting like a Jew or of acting like a gentile, but you can't accuse me of both at the same time. This proverbial utterance of the rabbi functions in the plot as it announces a theme of the text. Torah is incompatible with the sword, thus repeating the theme established through the typology of Esau, the Roman, and Jacob, the Jew.

This incompatability was apparently a Christian topos as well, as we learn from a story of Eusebius, the fourth-century historian who documented Christian martyrdom in Palestine. According to this source, a certain Roman soldier confessed himself a Christian and was given several hours to reconsider his confession or be martyred. "Meanwhile the bishop of Caesarea, Theotecnus, took hold of him and brought him near the altar. He raised a little the soldier's cloak and pointed to the sword, then pointed to the book of the gospels, and bade him choose between the two. The sword and the book are incompatible" (Lieberman 1939–1944, 445). This sensibility is, we suggest, particularly available to those who are in diaspora. Needless to say, once Christianity becomes imperial, this position must change, and by the fifth century, the sword is being imagined as a necessary concomitant of the book in the Church Dominant and the Church Militant.

As we will see, honesty is not the issue, for the rabbi is being disingenuous in the extreme here, and his dishonesty will be rewarded with a miracle. The point is rather to bring out the opposition between the Torah and modes of violence per se. The Romans ask him then:

> Why do they call you Rabbi [Master]? He answered them: "I am the master of the weavers." They brought before him two spools of thread and asked him: "Which is the warp and which is the woof?" A miracle took place for him. A male bee came and sat on the woof and a female bee came and sat on the warp.[36] "And why did you not come to the House of Abidan [the local pagan temple]?" He said: "I am old, and I was afraid that you would trample me with your feet." They said to him; "Up until now how many old men have been trampled?" A miracle took place for him, and that very day an old man was trampled.
>
> "Why did you release your slave to freedom?"[37]
>
> "It never happened!"
>
> One got up to testify against him [that he had released his slave]. Elijah came and appeared like one of them. He [the disguised Elijah] said to him [the potential witness]: "Since a miracle has happened for him in the other cases, a miracle will happen this time as well, and something bad will happen to you [literally, that man]."[38] That man [who was betraying him] did not pay attention and got up to tell them. A letter had been written to the House of Caesar. They sent it with him [the informer]. He [Elijah] threw him four hundred parasangs, so that he went and never came back.

This is a trickster tale par excellence. Rabbi El'azar the son of Perata repeatedly uses rhetorical methods involving "double meaning [and] ambiguous intentions," tactics that a Roman polemicist of the second Sophistic would deride as effeminate (Gleason 1995, 37).[39] The ironies of this rejection and of standing one's ground "like a man" and being martyred[40] are perhaps rendered even more palpable intertextually in that the rabbi's name, El'azar, was emblematic of the brave martyr. We can learn this from the apocryphon, 4 Maccabees, in which we read of the martyrdom of a namesake:

> After they had tied his arms on each side they cut him with whips, while a herald who faced him cried out, "Obey the king's commands!" But the courageous and noble man, like a true El'azar, was unmoved, as though being tortured in a dream; yet while the old man's eyes were raised to heaven, his flesh was being torn by scourges, his blood flowing, and his sides were being cut to pieces. Although he fell to the ground because his body could not endure the agonies, he kept his reason upright and unswerving. (6:3–7)

Our Rabbi El'azar is almost a parody of the "true El'azar," i.e., the upright and manly martyr who dies a "death with glory" (2 Maccabees 6:19), which Bowersock cogently describes as a "death as old as the *Iliad*" (1995, 11), rather than escape his fate through subterfuge.[41] As a parodic figure, the Rabbi El'azar of our story then represents a powerful critique of the ideology of death with honor that the Maccabean accounts encode.

In the typical fashion of the folk narrative, three miracles take place for our hero. In the first, after he has lied and declared himself the "rabbi" of the weavers, a professor of weaving, the Romans test him by showing him two spools of yarn and asking him to distinguish between the woof and the warp, that is, between the active and the passive, the male and the female thread. Miraculously, a male bee sits on the woof and a female bee on the warp, allowing the rabbi to convince the Romans that he is, indeed, a weaver. In the next miracle, Rabbi El'azar informs the Romans that the reason he does not attend the pagan worship (that is, the emperor worship) is because he is afraid of being trampled, and here as well a miracle takes place that convinces the Romans of the truth of his lie. Finally, a Jew is prepared to denounce the rabbi as having indeed freed his slave, which the story posits as both illegal and a sure mark of adherence to Judaism. Through a highly improbable combination of circumstances and miracles, the denouncer is removed so far from the scene that he will never be heard of again. We are in the realm of folk literature here, a genre whose presence here demonstrates the close connections between the rabbinic class and the "folk" (Hasan-Rokem 2000). The values of the story are clear as well. Any sort of deception is legitimate, as long as it gets you off the hook with the oppressor, because his rule is absolutely illegitimate. Our protagonist here is a veritable Brer Rabbi.

Following the comedy, the tragedy. Our next protagonist is anything but a trickster:

> They brought Rabbi Ḥanina the son of Teradion, and said to him: "Why did you engage in Torah?" He said to them: "For thus the Lord my God has commanded me!"
>
> They immediately sentenced him to burning, and his wife to execution [by the sword], and his daughter to sit in a prostitute's booth. . . .
>
> When the three of them were being taken out, they justified their verdicts. He said, "The Rock, His action is blameless" [Deut. 32:4], and his wife said, "He is a God of faithfulness and there is no wickedness. He is righteous and true" [Deut. 32:4], and his daughter said, "Your judgment is great and Your perception is manifold, for Your eyes are open to all of the ways of human beings" [to give each person according to his paths and the fruit of his wickedness] [Jeremiah 32:19]. Rabbi said: "How great are these three saints, for at the moment of justifying of God's judgment, there occurred to them the three verses of justification of the judgment."

This is an exemplary martyr story. Martyrdom is witness to the greater jurisdiction of God's power and justice that supersedes that of the mere temporal authority. Accordingly, when this rabbi is asked, "Why do you teach Torah?" he does not seek to evade an answer and thus culpability as his two predecessors in the text had done—both successfully—but defiantly admits to the "crime" and to the superiority of God's rule over him to that of the Roman ruler: "For thus the Lord my God has commanded me!" This admirable sentiment is the precise antithesis to that of Rabbi Eli‹ezer's duplicitous "I have trust in the J/judge."

Note the several readings of Rabbi Eli‹ezer's statement that are set in motion, particularly in contrast to the univocity of Rabbi Ḥanina's statements. "I have trust in the J/judge," first, is obviously intended to be (mis)understood by the Roman himself as a statement of trust in him. Second, it constitutes a statement on the part of Rabbi Eli‹ezer that he trusts in the Judge of the Universe that he will not be abandoned in his hour of trial and will be rescued, which in fact he is. But in the light of the antithetical echo story of Rabbi Ḥanina, we might begin to wonder if Rabbi Eli‹ezer's statement is, in fact, not a lie, not only with respect to the *hegemon* but with respect to the *Hegemon* as well. By seeking to escape the judgment that the Roman wishes to impose on him, is he not also seeking to escape the judgment that God wishes to impose on him—a judgment that would be justified (as in the case of Rabbi Ḥanina's family) by referring to the backsliding of Rabbi Eli‹ezer in the direction of heresy? The verdicts of Rabbi Ḥanina and his family are likewise justified both by the narrator and by the characters themselves. Perhaps Rabbi Eli‹ezer trusts *neither* judge (at least for the moment). Given our culture's predispositions toward honesty and martyrdom, we might very well understand that Rabbi Ḥanina's story is being presented as a hermeneutical key to reading the stories of both Rabbi Eli‹ezer and the farce of Rabbi El‹azar the son of Perata, and the latter two come off badly.

The text, however, immediately discredits such a reading in the sequel:

Our [ancient] Rabbis have taught: When Rabbi Yose the son
of Kisma became ill, Rabbi Ḥanina the son of Teradion went
to visit him. He said to him: "Ḥanina, my brother, Don't you
know that this nation was set to rule over us by Heaven, and
it has destroyed His house, and burned His temple, and killed
his saints, and destroyed his goodly things, and still it exists,
and I have heard that you gather crowds together in public,
with a Scroll of the Torah in your lap, and you sit and teach!"[42]
He [Ḥanina] said to him, "From Heaven they will have mercy."
He [Yose] said to him, "I say logical things to you, and you
answer me: 'From Heaven they will have mercy!' I will be surprised if they do not burn you and the Scroll of the Torah
with you."

Rabbi Yose here represents perfectly the pathos of diasporic
consciousness. Open resistance to domination by the imperial
power, by the dominant culture, would end not only in the
death of the Bad Jew but in the burning of his Scroll of the
Torah with him, easily read almost allegorically as the destruction of the possibility of continued study of Torah. The
only modes of resistance, in diaspora, that are logical, that
make sense, are those that will enable the continuation of that
cultural and spiritual activity. This passage is highly intelligible in the terms of Scott's analysis of the role of hidden transcripts and the social sites within which they are elaborated in
dominated communities. As he shows, in order for seditious
discourse to be formed, there have to be "autonomous social
sites" either hidden from the eyes of the dominating population or hidden from their ears because of "linguistic codes
impenetrable to outsiders" (1990, 127). The study of Torah
in sites such as the Bet Hamidrash, or even more in public
crowds, would provide such an arena, and it does not matter,
according to Scott, precisely what the discourse is in that
arena. Insofar as it maintains the possibility of a hidden transcript, of a place within which the dominated Jews could
elaborate their true views of their Roman (and in Babylonia,

Sassanian) overlords, it would serve the function. This is even more the case when the very content of Torah study incorporated encoded or open contempt for the rulers, as was, we suggest, frequently enough the case. The response of the "Romans," their efforts to prohibit the study of Torah (especially in crowds), would indicate their understanding—or perhaps only the understanding of those who tell the story, the Jews—of the role of such gatherings in the maintenance of the hidden transcript.

The text sends us some very ambivalent messages:

> They said: there did not pass many days until Rabbi Yose the son of Kisma died and all of the great of Rome went to bury him. On their way back, they found him [Rabbi Ḥanina] sitting and studying Torah and gathering congregations in public with the Scroll of the Torah placed in his lap. They wrapped him in the Scroll of the Torah and surrounded him with sticks of firewood and lit them and they brought wool swatches, soaked them in water, and placed them on his heart, in order that he not die quickly.

Rabbi Yose's prophecy came true exactly as predicted. The rabbi is burned along with the Scroll of the Torah. It was in a sense Rabbi Yose's accommodating practice (his conformity to the public transcript) that occasioned the tragedy. This text simply will not settle down in one place and take sides on the issue of accommodation versus resistance or on tricksterism versus martyrdom.

We can now go back and interpret a part of the narrative that we have left untouched until now. Immediately after describing the punishments of the three members of Rabbi Ḥanina's family, the text explains why God has allowed them to be so maltreated:

> "Him to burning": for he used to pronounce the Holy Name literally. How is it possible that he did such a thing? For we have a tradition that Abba Shaul says that also one who

pronounces the Holy Name literally has no place in the World to Come. He did it for the purpose of self-instruction, for as another tradition says: "'Do not learn to do' [pronouncing God's name; Deut. 18:9], but you may learn in order to understand and to teach." [If that is the case], why was he punished? Because he used to pronounce the Holy Name literally in public, and it says, "This is my eternal name" [Exodus 3:15], but the word "eternal" is spelt as if it meant "for hiding."

"And his wife for execution": because she did not censure him.

"And his daughter to sit in a prostitute's booth": for Rabbi Yoḥanan said: She was once walking among the great of Rome, and they said, "How beautiful are the steps of this maiden!" And she immediately became more careful about her steps. And this is what Resh Lakish has said: "The sin of my heels will ambush me" [Psalms 49:6]. The sins that a person steps out with his heels in this world will ambush him at the Judgment Day.

Exploration of the details of these explanations will strengthen the reading of gendered meanings in this text. Rabbi Ḥanina himself was condemned for doing something in public that he should have done in private. It was appropriate, indeed, for him to be pronouncing God's name as it is written and with its vowels in order to instruct himself (and according to the proof-text, in order to instruct others as well), but this activity needed to be carried out in private, *just as his study and teaching of Torah ought to have been in private, according to Rabbi Yose the son of Kisma*. God's name was given for hiding, not for public exposure to the eyes of the hostile Romans. In other words, the text is proposing a homology between the reasons for Rabbi Ḥanina's capture by the Romans at both the pragmatic and the ideological levels. The teaching of Torah is meant to be a private, internal activity for the Jewish people in a hostile world, a hidden transcript, and not a matter of provocation and defiance. Resistance, according to this particular rabbinic view, consists of doing what we do without getting into trouble and using evasiveness in order to keep doing it. Rabbi Ḥanina in defying the Romans was behaving in a way culturally intelligible to the Romans, while Rabbi Yose the son of Kisma by complying with the Romans *resisted* their cultural hegemony. "[The Romans] looked for the contest when one proclaimed one's *Nomen* or identity. The Romans, for instance, recognized that the man or woman who proclaimed *Christianus sum* or *Ioudaios eimi* were doing so as challenges" (Barton 1998). Rabbinic texts counseled Jews to disguise themselves as non-Jews in order to avoid being martyred (Theodor and Albeck 1965, 984).[43]

In other words, there is a certain contradiction between the narrative and the practice here. Rabbi Ḥanina's "story" is a story of resistance, but his practice is based on Roman models. He accedes, precisely through his defiance, to the values of those whom he would be resisting. On the other hand, Rabbi Yose's public narrative is one of accommodation. By doing so, however, he enables the continuation of Jewish cultural practice, in secret, and thus defies in two ways the cultural hegemony of the Romans. He does not accept their interpretation of manliness and honor—he resists it—and he facilitates the ongoingness of Jewish difference in the face of their demand that Jews "assimilate." The modern term is used here purposely, because the analogy to contemporary forms of Zionism is palpable. In resisting through becoming "Muscle Jews," it could be argued, the early Zionists were simply assimilating and capitulating to general European values (since "Muscular Christianity" was a dominant movement of that time as well), while through maintaining themselves as weak and passive, the Torah Jews of Eastern Europe were engaged in a more successful act of cultural resistance to the hegemony of Christian culture.

Rabbi Ḥanina's own sin, the sin of public provocation, is doubled by the sin of his daughter. Exposed to the predatory gaze of the powerful males of Rome, she does not evade the gaze but seeks to enhance her object-status further. Having thus rendered herself as a sexual object, she is punished by being turned into a whore, the ultimate depersonalized sexual object. Although the text is couched in the form of a critique of the woman, and that blaming of the victim ought not to be papered over in this reading, at the same time there is encoded here a critique of the male gaze itself. It is no accident that it is the important men of Rome who are represented at this moment; they are the proverbial (or stereotyped) "construction workers" for this text. Rashi comments, citing the verse of Proverbs: "A respectable king's daughter remains indoors." This key citation renders this story a virtual allegory for the existence of Israel among the nations, and particularly under the gaze of their Roman masters. We have here both a "sexist" demand for a kind of purdah for women and, since the daughter of the king is Israel herself, a comment on the proper behavior of Jews in the world. The approved practice for Jews is gendered feminine, while the behavior of the Roman is gendered masculine. The violence of their gaze is contiguous with the greater violence of their bloodshed, and the resistance of the Jew is to be veiled: "eternal" through being "in hiding," as the double meaning of the verse implies. Remain in the closet, as it were. Continue to live, continue to maintain Jewish practice, but do not behave in ways that draw attention or provoke the hostile intervention of the ruling powers. It is God who has sent them to rule. Thus the text ultimately endorses the view of Rabbi Yose the son of Kisma (and the practice of Rabbi El'azar ben Perata as well) but does not entirely erase or delegitimate the way of Rabbi Ḥanina either. Our impression is that this text seeks with all of its power to resist the notion of martyrdom but simply cannot, owing to the cultural prestige of the practice, directly and univocally condemn it.

The end of the daughter's story is once more highly illuminating:

Beruria, the wife of Rabbi Meʿir was the daughter of Rabbi Ḥanina. She said to him: "It is painful to me that my sister is sitting in a prostitute's booth." He took a *tarqeva* of dinars and went, saying if she has done nothing wrong [i.e., if she is sexually innocent], there will be a miracle, and if not, there will be no miracle. He dressed up as a soldier and solicited her. She said: "I am menstruating." He said: "I can wait." She said: "There are many here more beautiful than I." He said: "I understand from this that she has done nothing wrong." He went to her guard: "Give her to me!" The guard said: "I am afraid of the king." He [Meʿir] took the *tarqeva* of dinars, and gave it to him, and said: "Take the *tarqeva* of dinars. Keep half and use half for bribing anyone who comes." He [the guard] said: "What shall I do when they are gone?" He [Meʿir] said: "Say 'God of Meʿir save me' and you will be saved." He [the guard] said: "How do I know that this will be so?" He [Meʿir] said: "[Now you will see.]" There came some dogs that eat people. He shouted to them, and they came to eat him [the guard]. He said: "God of Meʿir save me," and they let him go. He let her go.[44]

The daughter of Rabbi Ḥanina bluffs her way out of the situation. All that is necessary for God to perform miracles and for her to be saved is that she succeed at the task. The "dishonorable" means are totally irrelevant. At the same time, however, the text highlights the vulnerability of the people without power. Without the miracle, they would be eaten alive by the "dogs." Furthermore, the text makes clear that the counsel of tricksterism is intended not only for women.

The matter became known in the house of the king. They brought him [the guard] and crucified him. He said "God of Meʿir save me," and they took him down and asked: "What was that?" He told them: "This is how the events took place." They wrote it on the gates of the city, and they engraved Rabbi Meʿir's face on the gates of Rome and said: "If a man who looks like this comes, arrest him!" When Rabbi Meʿir came there, they wished to arrest him. He ran away from them and *went into a whorehouse.* Elijah came in the guise of a whore and embraced him. Some say that he put his hand in gentile foods and tasted them. They [the Romans] said: "God forfend! If that were Rabbi Me'ir he wouldn't do such a thing." Because of these events [Rabbi Me'ir] ran away to Babylonia.

The most striking aspect of this sequence is, of course, the escape via entering into the whorehouse and, moreover, disguising himself, once more, as a customer of the prostitutes. This time, however, it is not to test the chastity of someone else but to save his own skin. Just, however, as it was considered by the Jewish text entirely proper for the young woman to pretend to acquiescence in prostitution in order to preserve her life, so it is entirely proper for Rabbi Me'ir to disguise himself and pretend to (or maybe actually) violate the Jewish law in order to keep himself alive. This is in accord with the principle that there are only three sins for which a Jew is required to give up his or her life to avoid: idol worship, murder, and incest. Rabbi Me'ir runs away to Babylonia, the safer place for the study of Torah, and not so incidentally the place where this story was formulated. In the end, then, there is a perfect analogy between the male rabbi and the young female Jew, and in addition the thematic material of the entire text is brought together in a culminating fashion. Both are to survive within the diaspora situation through the maintenance of moral purity and Jewish identity, but both are to do so precisely through dissimulation, through trickery. The text opens up to its final moral and nearly allegorical meanings in which the Jewish People is figured no more as a man, Jacob, but as a woman.

As Laurie Davis has strikingly phrased it, "the Rabbis see themselves as virgins in a brothel" (1994). Her argument, paraphrased, runs as follows: the brothel is a dangerous place—the place of diaspora—and a place of testing within which Jewish men and women can prove their purity. "After proof is delivered, the brothel is transformed into a safe haven where Jews can harmlessly pretend assimilation"; in other words it is safe to *pretend* to accede to the public transcript. When the situation becomes, however, intolerable, then the appropriate solution is to run away. "From the preceding stories, it is clear that it is the Rabbis *themselves* who felt keenly the difficulty of remaining pure in an impure world. They fear pollution and assimilation. In this over-determined fantasy, the Rabbis act out the roles of both oppressor and oppressed, powerful and victimized, the assimilated and the vulnerable." Davis declares, then, that she sees "female characters in this story as the personification of men at their most vulnerable. My feminist reading counters traditional feminist interpretation which posits women as other and consistently objectified. Beruriah and her sister are what Luce Irigaray calls the 'pseudo-other': alternate male identities, aspects which men project outward. In this case, we suggest what the Rabbis wish to disown is their vulnerability which women so readily symbolize." There is one way that we would seriously revise this conclusion, however, one that goes to the heart of the evaluation of diaspora as a cultural strategy and as a cultural condition. Rather than seeing the Rabbis as abjecting their vulnerability through the figure of the woman who remains pure in the brothel, here at least we would see them as identifying with that female figure. The brothel within which they remain pure is the brothel of the Roman Empire with its temptations of heresy, prostitutes, and the government.[45]

Diaspora and the Critique of the Phallic Male

Rabbinic culture has always been a diasporized and dominated culture, one that subsisted within political and social conditions in which another culture was dominant and hegemonic. In antiquity and throughout cultural history, the rabbinic discourse of masculinity was in a complex relation of attraction/rejection with the "dominant fiction" of the hegemonic formation of the larger cultures of which the Jews were a part. Even though a case can be made that the diasporic modes of ideal masculinity are more pronounced in Babylonia than in Palestine of the Talmudic period, this distinction is only relative. In Palestine as well, the Jews of this time were in diaspora. Jews knew about "the phallus"; it was all around them as a mode of representing maleness.[46] As such, it was an object of enormous attraction, as well as one of repulsion, a figure of desired prestige and power, but also of hideous violence. As Carlin Barton has recently written, "Not everyone in the [Roman] culture idolized the gladiator, or envied, or acted cruelly. However, I do think that these behaviors were sufficiently common in the period of the late Republic and the early Empire as to merit explanation from even the most reverent student" (1993, 7). Thomas Wiedemann makes a similar point when he discusses a terra-cotta statuette that represents a particularly horrible execution by beasts and remarks, "The emotions which induced someone to keep such a terracotta model in his home are not ones that we can easily share, but they should not be dismissed as aberrant" (1992, 82). Analogously, there must have been many cruel Jews in late antiquity, and even more to the point, there must have been cruel rabbis as well, but the *discourse* of the Rabbis to a great extent was oriented toward opposition to cruelty and violence.

Throughout much of the culture that we call Western, male sexuality itself has been understood as normally and normatively violent. As a recent critic has written of the fin-de-siècle English sexologist Havelock Ellis, one of the consequences of the "dominant fiction" of gender in our culture involves the patronizing assumption that "men whose deepest sexual desire does not involve dominance of women [i.e., rape] must be in some way physically deficient." Ellis considers "the hymen an anatomical expression of that admiration of force which marks the female in her choice of a mate" (Siegel 1995, 59; Craft 1995, 90). A very recent writer—a psychoanalyst—continues to reflect this ideology of maleness by assuming confidently that "strength, assertiveness, activity, stoicism, courage, and so forth" are "gender syntonic" for men (Lane 1986, 147). In this, he continues the common wisdom of a culture within which a novelist could write:

> Hermenia was now beginning to be so far influenced by Alan's personality that she yielded the point with reluctance to his masculine judgement. It must always be so. The man must needs retain for many years to come the personal hegemony he has usurped over the woman; and the woman who once accepts him as lover or as husband must give way in the end, even in matters of principle, to his virile self-assertion. She would be less a woman, he less a man, were any other result possible. Deep down in the very roots of the idea of sex we come on that prime antithesis—the male, active and aggressive; the female, sedentary, passive, and receptive.[47]

And as that consummate representative of Victorian culture John Ruskin wrote, "The man's power is active, progressive, defensive. He is eminently the doer, the creator, the discoverer, the defender. His intellect is for speculation and invention; his energy for adventure, for war, and for conquest," while women "must be enduringly, incorruptibly, good; instinctively, infallibly wise—wise, not for self-development, but for self-renunciation . . . wise, not with the narrowness of insolent and loveless pride, but with the passionate gentleness of an infinitely variable, because infinitely applicable, modesty of service."[48] Thomas Luxon cites several examples from English literature within which images of warfare, and indeed rape, are central to valorized descriptions of male "love," such as Sidney's "Astrophil and Stella" and John Donne's "Batter My Heart." As Luxon strikingly remarks, "Violence *is* foreplay in the misogynist imaginary" (1995). Maria Ramas has connected Freud's "Primal Scene" of parental intercourse as a scene of sadomasochistic violence with the peculiar sexual fantasies of Victorian culture. Citing studies of the pornography of this period, she concludes: "Psychoanalytic theory argues that the phantasy of the 'primal scene' is in fact a *mis*-interpretation on the child's part, due to the influence of a specific libidinal phase—the anal-sadistic stage. In contrast, we believe it is an accurate perception of the dominant patriarchal sexual phantasy. The phantasy, quite simply, expresses erotically the essential meaning of sexual difference in patriarchal culture" (1980, 482). Ramas quite correctly, in my opinion, connects the structure of this fantasy with "the phallus," showing that the violent scenes of heterosexual initiation that were virtually ubiquitous in Victorian pornography are all connected with a peculiar form of phallus worship, "'Nature's grand masterpiece, the pillar of ivory,' the 'terrible engine,' 'the ravishing instrument' that in ripping the woman apart inspires her admiration and awe. Its potency, affirmed through violence, seduces her and gives her pleasure" (Craft 1995, 89). The question that arises, however, is whether this representation of male sexuality as sadomasochistic violence is the "essential meaning of sexual difference in patriarchal culture," or, perhaps, the essential meaning of sexual difference in certain patriarchal cultures, indeed whether there might not be other cultures, equally patriarchal, equally male dominant, within which male sexuality is not imagined as violent and predatory.

Ramas specifies precise material and social conditions under which violent and dominating models of intercourse would develop (501–2), conditions that by no means obtain in all patriarchies. These conditions include a situation in which there is one extremely dominating class of males, whether economically or ethnically based. Conditions of imperial domination, as in Rome (Brooten 1996, II.A.1) or the Victorian age, within which a group of men dominate immense spaces and populations, would only enhance such developments.[49]

The problem is that Ramas describes and projects society exclusively from the position of the dominant class. If, as Ramas claims, "gender and class, femininity and service, were at the same time conflated," then the question of the subjectivity of the dominated male becomes central.

Through studying early Christian and Jewish texts, we can begin to suggest at least a tentative and partial answer to this question, namely, that even for those men "on the bottom," being there was indeed interpreted as femminization, but femminization itself was transvalued and received at least some positive significance. Jewish culture in Europe seriously threatens the universal validity of Ramas's claims. Gender is historically and materially determined. As we begin to look at the Jewish culture of late antiquity, we can begin to construct a genealogy for the nineteenth-century antiphallicism of European Jewish culture and its resistance to the culture of violent male sexuality that was endemic, even acutely so at this time (Dijkstra 1986).

The very conditions that Ramas determines as productive of violent male sexuality did not obtain in a rabbinic society within which the speaking males of the texts were not culturally, politically, or economically dominant vis-à-vis their imperial overlords, the Roman and Sassanid empires, and within themselves belonged to different socioeconomic classes, from landed aristocracy to small craftsmen to the peasantry. Indeed, the class instability and cross-class solidarities, perhaps, of dominated, diasporic populations might very well be correlated with certain modes of cultural creativity as well. Similarly for early Christianity, which stood in antagonism to imperial power, there are textual and other practices that suggest strongly that neither patriarchy nor the phallus are constants. Until now, this has frequently been represented as the sign of a lack, of a "castration" of the early Christian and the premodern Jew. As Thomas Luxon phrased the question: "Isn't this simply to suggest that, deprived of political phallic power and conscious of that deprivation, masculinity and the penis, and indeed, gender itself will always appear very different? Politically deprived of the phallus, the penis is 'just' a penis? Might this also account for the anti-allegorical ethos of dominated peoples, cultures, sects [e.g., the early Protestant Reformation]? When the dominant fiction says you are a woman, you try to reject the dominant fiction" (1995).

Luxon has here precisely formulated the perspective that this book sets out to reverse, a perspective that in Jewish historiography has become known as the "lachrymose" conception of Jewish history. We claim that the absence of *phallic* power is not a lack. It need not be figured as a castration, as psychoanalysis figures the woman and the circumcised Jew, but as a gain, as a place from which a particular knowledge is generated. Such a position has been articulated by Jewish thinkers before, but not often.[50] Interestingly, and perversely, the *lack* of such positioned knowledge, gay savoire, to appropriate David Halperin's terms, this very "stupidity *(das Radikal-Dumme)*" was considered by some, including some Jews, to be an asset that Jews lacked (Hoberman 1995, 152–53)!

Where European aristocratic culture despised the submissive male, both early Christian and early Jewish cultures frequently valorized "him."[51] Both early rabbinic Jews and early Christians performed resistance to the Roman imperial power structure through "gender-bending," thereby marking their own understanding that gender itself is implicated in the maintenance of political power. Thus various symbolic enactments of "femaleness"—as constructed within a particular system of genders—among them asceticism, submissiveness, retiring to private spaces, and circumcision (interpreted in a distinctive way, which I will discuss later) were adopted variously by Christians or Jews as acts of resistance against the Roman culture of masculinist power wielding.[52]

Esau versus Jacob: The Mirror of the Other

> Biblical fathers, it would seem, are not made for the Freudian masterplot.
>
> — Y. S. Feldman, "'And Rebecca Loved Jacob,' but Freud
> Did Not"

For the midrash, Esau and Jacob are typological paradigms for Rome and Israel respectively. The images of masculinity that are projected in the rabbinic readings of these two figures provide important clues to the rabbinic projections and constructions of their own male selves, of their own selves as "masculine." Esau, the biblical ancestor of Edom, represents for the Rabbis the type of the "Roman," who is, throughout rabbinic literature, the privileged other of the Jew, functioning in a way analogous to the figure of the Scythian who defines by contrast the Greek in the writings of Herodotus (Hartog 1988). In the latter case, however, it was precisely the lack of a homeland that made the Scythian nomads a defining other for the Greeks, while, for the Jews, it is the Romans' imperial domination over *them* that puts them into that position. Both of these instances help us glimpse the links among imperialism, colonization, and diaspora.

It should be emphasized, of course, that (virtually) nothing can be learned about "real Romans" from this literature. The "Romans," by the same or any other name, function here as the mirror over/against which the Rabbis formulate their own sense of identity and paradigms for human and especially male behavior.

The very biblical verse that sets up the typology of these two brothers sets the scene as well for the cultural construction of the sexuality of the aggressive "Roman" male versus the Jewish nomadic, diasporic male: "And the boys grew up, and Esau was a hunter, a man of the field, and Jacob was an innocent, a dweller in tents" (Gen. 25:27). From this verse we see that the self-representation of Israel—for so Jacob is renamed and thus becomes the eponym of the nation—as different in his gendering (even though both are referred to as "men") from Esau is adumbrated in the Bible and is not only a product of a crisis generated by the condition of political powerlessness. In addition to describing Jacob as a "dweller in tents," the prototypical female space, and Esau as a "man of the field" and a hunter, it also clearly associates Jacob with femaleness by indicating that his mother preferred him, while his father preferred the masculine Esau: "And Isaac loved Esau, because he had game in his mouth, while Rebecca loved Jacob" (25:28). This binary opposition was thus available to the Rabbis as a positive and culturally internal resource for a self-fashioning within the situation of domination by the Romans. Of course, the Rabbis, through their midrash, subtly and powerfully mobilized this typology in specific directions. Most prominently, it was the reading of Jacob's "tent" as the House of Study that effected this mobilization.[53]

In a passage from the definitive late antique midrash on Genesis, *Bereshit Rabba,* we find an initial picture of the general rabbinic constructions of their own masculinity in the mirror of the other, the "Roman." We begin to find such male self-fashioning at the very opening of the midrash on the Torah portion known in Hebrew as "generations" (Gen. 25:19ff.):

> "One who begets a wise son will be joyful with him" (Prov. 23:24): Rabbi Huna said in the name of Rabbi Aḥa, "From where do you know that anyone who has a son who labors in Torah is filled with love for him; therefore it teaches [talmud lomar]: 'My son, if your heart is wise, my heart will be joyful'" (Prov. 23:16). Rabbi Shimʿon the son of Menassia says, "From this I would know only that his flesh-and-blood father is joyful; from where that also the Holy, Blessed One is filled with love for him at the hour that he labors in Torah; therefore [the verse] continues 'I also.'" (Theodor and Albeck 1965, 678)

This meditation is presented in the midrash as an initial gloss on the verse: "These are the generations of Isaac the son of Abraham, Abraham begat Isaac" (Gen. 25:19). In other words, the first point that the text wishes to make about male succession is what sort of son is desired by the normative father of rabbinic tradition, and that is, not surprisingly, a son learned in Torah. No other male role or characteristic is discussed or contemplated as desirable. Strikingly, moreover, the language of this midrashic passage is suffused with eroticism. The passage in Proverbs speaks apparently about the father being happy that such a child has been born to him, but the midrashic text reads "will be joyful with him" in another, stronger sense, more like the sense that the phrase carries when it is in the context of a bridegroom being happy with his bride. The father is not presented as being proud of the son but of being filled with love for him at the moment of the son's engagement with Torah. Mutual attachment to the (female) Torah shared by these men produces representations of strong homosocial bonds between them, bonds that are occasionally symbolized in the texts via the connections between them produced through marriage to actual women as well. This raises, of course, the interesting question of whether Jewish women had a diaspora. Moreover, the bond between the divine father and the human son is also presented in these eroticized terms. God also is filled with love for the son when the latter is engaged in the study of Torah.

We will look quite closely at two narratives, the common thread of which is the constitution of a homosocial couple in which one of the male partners is figured as "wife" to the other, and this wifeliness is projected as a paradigm for male deportment. The argument that we wish to make is that such imagination of masculinity as dependent, with all the positive and negative social effects that such an imagination can carry with it, is a peculiar cultural effect of the condition of men in diaspora (whether that diaspora be ethnic, religious, racial, or even sexual in its origins).

The Emperor "Wife"

The first text is a story that occurs as part of a cycle of tales about the relations between Rabbi Yehudah Hannassi, known simply as Rabbi, the political and religious leader of the Palestinian Jews under Roman rule, and the Caesar, Antoninus son of Severus. We have, therefore, a paradigmatic situation of the representation of Jewish and Roman masculine ideals, from the Jewish point of view, of course. At the point that we enter the tale, after having been regaled with the Rabbi's great wisdom and how he and the Caesar became great friends and the Rabbi became a trusted adviser to the Roman ruler,[54] we are informed:

> Every day [Antoninus Caesar] used to serve Rabbi. He used to feed him and give him drink. When Rabbi wished to get up on his bed, [Antoninus] would kneel down before the bed and say: "Get up on me to your bed." [Rabbi] said: "It is not appropriate to demean the kingship so." [Antoninus] said: "May I be a couch under you in the Next World!" [Antoninus] said: "Will I come into the Next World?" [Rabbi] said: "Yes." [Antoninus] said, but is it not written: "There will not be a remnant left of the house of Esau" [Obadiah 1:18]? "That applies only to one who behaves as Esau." [Antoninus] said, but is it not written: "Edom is destroyed with its kings and all of its princes" [Ezekiel 32:29]? "Its kings—but not all of its kings! All of its princes—but not all of its ministers!"
>
> There is also a tannaitic tradition that says this: "Its kings—but not all of its kings! All of its princes—but not all of its ministers! Its kings, but not all of its kings, that is, except for Antoninus the son of Severus. All of its princes but not all of its ministers, that is, except for Keṭiʿa bar Shalom."
>
> And what is this story of Keṭiʿa bar Shalom?
>
> There was a certain Caesar who hated Jews. He said to his courtiers: "If someone has a wart on his leg, should he cut it off and live or leave it and suffer?"
>
> They said to him: "Let him cut it off and live!"
>
> Keṭiʿa bar Shalom said to him: "First of all, you won't be able to defeat all of them, for it is written, 'I have scattered them as the four winds of the heavens' [Zachariah 2:10]— What is this 'as the four winds'? It ought to read 'to the four winds'! Rather it means that just as the world cannot exist without winds, so the world cannot exist without Israel. And secondly, they will call you a king who cuts."

[Caesar] said: "You have spoken well, but anyone who defeats the king [in argument] gets thrown into a hollow furnace."

When they were taking him out [to be executed], a certain Matron said to him: "Woe to the ship that goes without the toll!"

He fell on the end of his foreskin and bit it off. He said: "I have paid the toll, and I will pass."

A voice was heard [from Heaven]: "Ḳeṭiʻa bar Shalom is invited to the Next World!" Rabbi cried and said: "There are those who acquire the next world in one instant, and those who acquire the next world only after many years!"

Antoninus served Rabbi, and when Antoninus died, Rabbi said: "The tie is rent!" (Avoda Zara 10b, following ms. JTS Rabbinowitz 15)

Reading this text will provide us with important insights into rabbinic self-fashioning on several levels. In its function as wish fulfillment, this kind of text has something like the force of dreams in Freudian theory (Kristeva 1986, 41). The most obviously dreamlike aspect of the story is the fantasy of the Roman emperor who serves as a footstool for the spiritual leader of the Jews. The way that this particular fantasy is played out in the story is much richer than mere revenge, however. In fact, what is thematized in this text is both a presentation of a stereotyped "Esau" or "Edom," i.e., Rome in rabbinic symbolism, as well as a partial interruption of that stereotype through the recognition of exceptions to it. As we shall see, the two consecutive episodes that we have excerpted here from the larger narrative sequence double each other in their presentation of the "Roman" versus the "Jew."

At first glance, the political and religious meanings of these stories seem quite obvious, almost to the point of triviality. A subject and displaced people (this story is about Palestine and Roman rule but told in Babylonia!) fantasizes two forms of reversal of its subjugation: one, that the very leaders of the dominating political power will become subject to the leaders of the dominated group (compare Jean Genet's *The Blacks* and *The Maids*) and the other, that God Himself will reward the subjected population in the next world with a much greater benefit than that which the tyrants enjoy in the present world. By treating the two stories as mirrors of each other, however, a rich reading of the role of gender and power and their symbolic connection with circumcision in rabbinic culture begins to develop. In the first episode, the Rabbi and the Caesar, the gendered meanings are quite palpable. This Caesar is an exception to the general rule that kings of "Esau" have no place in the next world by virtue of his sympathetic treatment of the Jews. The way that he earns this exceptional status is, however, fascinating. He becomes socially—if not sexually—Rabbi's wife. The services that he performs for Rabbi, preparing food and drink for him and even, in displaced fashion, preparing his bed for him, all strongly mark him as the female partner in a marriage. According to Babylonian Talmud Ketubbot 96a, in fact, preparing his drink and his bed are two of the three most intimate services that the wife is expected to perform for her husband.[55] These are explicitly coded as intimate and erotic in import, since it is these that are forbidden during her menstrual period in order to prevent any possibility that husband and wife will inadvertently be swept away into sexual passion (61a). Furthermore, of all of the kinds of work that a widow is expected to perform for her husband's heirs while she is being supported by his estate (grinding, baking, laundering, cooking, and woolwork), giving them drink and making their beds are once more explicitly excluded (96a). This indicates the particularly intimate and conjugal nature of these activities, and it is these that Antoninus performs for Rabbi. This performance wins him his exceptional place among all Roman rulers in the next world. This femminization of Antoninus is again strongly signified by Antoninus's desire to be "bedding" for Rabbi in the next world. In addition, according to the Babylonian Talmud

(Yevamot 62b), the wife is described in this world as a "mattress for her husband," and, in the next world, it is the reward of the virtuous wife to serve as his footstool. Finally, the strongly homoeroticized character of this imaginary friendship is inscribed in Rabbi's lament on the death of Antoninus, "The tie is rent," glossed forthrightly by Rashi as "Our love which has joined us soul to soul." A homoerotic relationship in antiquity always inscribes one of the partners as gendered female. The overly "male" Roman emperor becomes righteous and earns his place in the next world through femminization. This femminization is thus positively marked within the culture, and this cannot be only for Roman men. If acting as a "wife" toward important scholarly men is what gets Roman men into the next world, then it is even more the case for Jewish men. Indeed, one point of the story is precisely to present that model of "feminine" service and homoerotic attachment as a male ideal, and the Talmudic text is addressed, of course, to Jews.

Moreover, this "wifely" ideal as the proper relationship of student to master is explicitly coded in the texts. The ideal rabbinic disciple is described as "washing the teacher's hands"—indeed, this is a common metaphor for "He was the Rabbi's disciple"—and sure enough, washing the husband's hands and face is the third of the most intimate services of the wife to the husband that the menstruant is forbidden to perform. As servile as this position is, it is nevertheless positively marked for both men and women within the culture, just as a "feminized" servility was receiving positive valorizations within Christian culture at about the same time. It is a figure for renunciation/rejection/disavowal of the phallus. We do not, of course, claim that such servility had the same meanings for men as for women. Indeed, it could be argued that the adoption of femininity by men in a culture within which there is a major disparity in power between the genders (virtually all human culture until now) will always form an appropriation, a virtual "theft" of femaleness.[56] Tania Modleski has well put it by referring to "how frequently male subjectivity works to appropriate 'femininity' while oppressing women" (1991, 7). This does not, however, exhaust the meaning that such valorization of submission has within culture, nor does it eradicate the differences between cultures within which submission was despised and only domination prized and cultures within which submissiveness was valued.

An effective ground to this figure of a valorized submissiveness, of an emotional dependence of men on men, can be garnered from Roman texts. When Cicero wishes to attack Antony, he first accuses him of having been a prostitute, and then: "but soon Curio turned up, drew you away from your meretricious trade and, as if he had given you a matron's robe, established you in lasting and stable matrimony. No boy bought for sexual gratification was ever so much in the power of his master as you were in Curio's" (Edwards 1993, 64). Catherine Edwards, in citing this passage, makes the excellent point that what offends here is not primarily the sexual practice, for as she says, "Cicero contrives to make a stable, lasting relationship sound far more reprehensible than prostitution," and this because "Antony's emotional attachment to Curio, he implies, reduced him to a position of slave-like dependence" (64–65). It was the dependence of one man on another, emotionally and materially, that was considered shameful rather than their sexual practices. We have here the founding moments of a culture characterized recently by Lee Edelman as one in which there is "a deeply rooted concern about the possible meanings of dependence on other males" (50).[57] The "good" Roman emperor, according to this Jewish legend, not only allowed himself to be dependent on the leading rabbinic sage of his day but even behaved toward him as a wife toward a husband, and this is how he earned his place in the world to come.

We are now in a position to read the even more symbolic story of Ḳeṭiʿa bar Shalom, who also, by being an exception and explicitly marked as such, defines what the stereotype of "Roman" is and, even more to the point, what the self-definition of Jewishness is. We are going to read this story as an echo of the previous one. This echoing effect is supported by two moments within the narrative: first, the explicit antithetical notice of Ķeṭiʻa bar Shalom as the servant of a Caesar who "hates the Jews," evidently in opposition to Antoninus, the Caesar who loves the Jews; and second, in the activity of stooping in order to circumcise himself that enables him to pass. The act of stooping and mutilating his phallus is what provides the possibility for Ķeṭiʻa bar Shalom (whose name is obviously emblematic, "The Cut One, Son of Peace") to pass the tollgate and enter into the next world, an ironic reflection of the Roman toll-gatherer who would normally prevent the subject populations from passing without paying the toll. This reading is doubled by the puns on the Hebrew root *ķṭʻ*, "to cut." The Caesar considers the Jews to be a painful blemish on his realm and wishes to cut them out, as one would cut out a wart. Ķeṭiʻa bar Shalom warns him (citing chapter, verse, and midrash of course!) both that he will not be able to succeed at that aim (Jewish wish fulfillment) and that he will then be stereotyped as a "cutter." The term that Ķeṭiʻa bar Shalom uses to indicate the way that the king will be stereotyped is, however, precisely his name, which also means (in the passive voice), the cut one, i.e., the circumcised one. "Cutter" is thus structurally opposed to "Cut One," as evil (the bad king who hates Jews) to good (the righteous gentile who saves Jews). What we propose, therefore, is that in addition to whatever other meanings this legend encodes, if we read it in the light of its immediate context, it also thematizes and valorizes femminization. Gentile attainment of the next world via circumcision, that which every Jewish male undergoes, consists of the same kind of symbolic femminization that was encoded explicitly in the story of Antoninus and Rabbi, and that Ķeṭiʻa bar Shalom also stooped to conquer.

It should be noted that Ķeṭiʻa bar Shalom's self-circumcision has no halakic (normative) status. He has not thereby converted to Judaism, nor, in fact, was it necessary for him to be circumcised in order to achieve a place in the next world; he could have done so under the rubric of righteous gentile, which he clearly was. Moreover, the act is proposed in the text, ironically enough, not by a Jewish voice at all, but by a *matrona,* a figure for Roman culture within Babylonian Jewish texts like this one.[58] Once more, the text is proposing here a self-construction through the eyes of a gentile character, looking, as it were, at Jews. We do not have here, then, a representation of the "official" meanings of circumcision, but of public, nonofficial, and even perhaps unarticulated meanings. They are all the more significant for that. Given the echoes and doubling from the previous story in the context, both the act of submission and perhaps the mutilation of the genital itself and the concurrent bleeding seem possibly to have had femminizing significances.

In Roman literature this femminization through circumcision appeared as a thoroughly negative representation. In Petronius, the slave with the intact foreskin is the more "virile" lover (Daniel 1979). Moreover, among the acts of molding of the male infant's body that a nurse is expected to perform in order to thoroughly virilize him is stretching his foreskin should it seem undeveloped. The short foreskin, then, was among the other signs of an effeminate nature (Gleason 1995, 71), and the intentional removal of the foreskin could only have been read as perverse. An analogy will help understand this point. Epictetus, in his *Discourses,* writes, "Nature made women smooth and men hirsute. If a man born hairless is an ominous sign *(teras),* what are we to make of a man who depilates himself (3.1.27–28)" (Gleason 1995, 69). Since making oneself less male on purpose through depilation was considered perverse, and the long foreskin was considered a sign of masculinity, circumcision, a deliberate "feminization"— in the very terms of their own cultural construction of the foreskin—would have seemed to these Romans just as perverse as depilation. Within Jewish culture, we suggest, the same

representation, circumcision as femminizing, became positively marked. This complements the transvaluation of femminizing servility that we read in the first episode of the text.

There is important support for this notion from the reading of the famous verse of Ezekiel in which Israel is figured as
a female child (16:6). God says to her, "I found you weltering
in your blood," and blesses her, "Live in your blood." This female blood is interpreted in rabbinic literature as the male
blood of circumcision.[59] This displacement involves very
complicated semiotic transactions. Israel is female partner
with respect to God, but many of the adepts in Israel are
male. An event must take place in their bodies that will enable
them to take the position of the female, and that event is circumcision. Ezekiel's metaphor of weltering in one's blood
becomes the vehicle for a transformation of male blood into
female blood and thus of male Israelites into female. This
transformation is powerfully enacted at the ritual level, until
today, when at a traditional circumcision ceremony, the newly
circumcised boy is addressed: "And I say to you [feminine]: In
your [feminine] blood, you [feminine] shall live. And I say to
you [feminine]: In your [feminine] blood, you [feminine] shall
live." These texts suggest strongly the possibility that circumcision was understood somehow as rendering to the male
something of the attributes of the female,[60] thus making it
possible for the male Israelite to have erotic communion with
a male deity within a homoerotic economy in which one partner must always be femminized. We are suggesting, therefore,
that there is here further evidence for a valorization of such
femminization.[61] Our argument is that it is as unsatisfactory
to conclude that this valorization is "mere" appropriation of
femaleness as it would be to see some feminist feeling here. It
is neither and both. On the one hand, there is clearly an ap-
propriative move within the rabbinic culture for men to take
over, or at any rate to append themselves to, women in the
processes of procreation unique to the female body, but at the
same time, there is a critical move against masculinism being

made here, against definitions of manliness as privation of that which is feminine. The Talmudic text that we will read in the next section is sharply critical of the appropriation of women implicated in this "feminism" at the same time that it also insists on the worth of the femminization itself.

This story and analysis begin to give us some insight into rabbinic collective male self-construction in diasporic conditions. The ideal Jew is portrayed in contrast to a stereotyped Roman other who is depicted as violent and cruel in his masculinity. At the same time, however, the stereotype is complicated by allowing that there are exceptions even among the Romans, Romans who are more like us, and their more-like-us-ness is figured as femminization. In fact, as Maud Gleason has recently made eminently clear, manliness was a highly contested quality for the Romans also; that is, every male (nearly) wanted to be manly—the question was precisely how it was constituted.[62] This explicit marking of the exception ("Its kings—but not all of its kings") reinforces the stereotype, but also marks the narrative of proper male behaviors and relationships as appropriations of the "feminine." Crucial to our argument, of course, is the assumption that we should not read this story as a mere fantasy of reversal of status, with Jews now "on top," a reading that would leave the representations of gender exactly where they were, i.e., in modern terms, one that would still privilege "top" over "bottom." Against such a reading stands the fact that according to another Talmudic legend, Rabbi himself, this same religious and political leader of Palestinian Jewry, had also to become "female" through a painful mimesis of the pain of childbirth in order to achieve his true destination as nurturing—not conquering—hero (D. Boyarin 1994, "Jewish Masochism").

We think a good case can be made that the Rabbis represented Roman maleness as aggressively phallic, which may say nothing about Roman culture but nevertheless is significant for describing the culture of the Rabbis. This raises the important theoretical issue in cultural studies of the stereotype (Bhabha 1983). Ultimately the point that needs to be emphasized is that this is *not* a discussion of real differences between Roman/tic and Jewish male behavior but about different cultural models signified in large part in specular, mutually confirming stereotypes. Thus, while Jewish men are represented by European Christian culture as feminized, they in turn represented the "goy" as crude, violent, macho, hypermale (D. Boyarin 1997, 33–80). The stereotypes seem to confirm each other, to agree with each other that the Jewish male lacks the phallus that the gentile possesses and thus to propose a homology between political and sexual domination. This topos was to remain active throughout Jewish history and right into modernity. The situation of the European diaspora male Jew as politically disempowered produced a sexualized interpretation of him as queer, because political passivity was in the Roman world equated precisely with effeminacy (Wiedemann 1992, 37). In modernity, this became reconfigured as homosexuality. As John Fout has written, "The male homosexual was portrayed as sickly, effeminate, perverse, and out of control, just the opposite of the 'normal' male, who was physically strong and active, the head of the family, dominant in the public world of politics at home and abroad, and in complete control of his sexuality and his emotions. The male homosexual only personified female characteristics, such as passivity and physical and emotional weaknesses" (1992, 413). These "female characteristics" are, as well, the very characteristics that were identified as belonging to the Jew—by anti-Semites and Zionists. Diaspora is essentially queer, and an end to diaspora would be the equivalent of becoming straight. The fact, then, that political Zionism was invented precisely at the time of the invention of heterosexuality is entirely legible. The dominant male of Europe, the "Aryan," is the one who is already "physically strong and active, the head of the family, dominant in the public world of politics at home and abroad," and thus not queer, so an assimilation that would lend the male Jew these characteristics would accomplish the same heterosexualizing project as Zionism.

Something else, however, must be emphasized here as well. Virtually all of the texts discussed here represent the goy not by depicting a gentile but by depicting a Jew who is, in some wise, like "them"—or, as in the case of our story, a goy who is like us. This is a double-edged sword, but an interesting one. On the one hand, it interrupts a simply racist notion: *We* are not like *them*. On the other hand, by inscribing the negative pole as "goyishness," there is a reinscription of an essentialized negative stereotype of "their" culture. It is as offensive when all evil in Jews is referred to as their being "like goyim" as it is when some Christians or Otto Weininger refer to evil in gentiles as having a Jewish character. It cannot be denied that this "racist" mood overtakes Jewish culture more than occasionally, for instance in the Yiddish proverb: *Alle Yevonim hobm ein ponim* (All Greeks/Ivans have one face [Funkenstein 1995, 1]). Nonetheless, we would argue that it is not an essentialized goyishness that is being stereotyped so much as a particular European cultural formation of masculinity.[63]

This formation was resisted from within European (Christian) culture as well, notably by celibates and celibacy, as if to grant that male sexuality is violent and aggressive by nature and the only way to renounce such violence is by renouncing, as it were, masculinity itself (Burrus 1995, "Reading Agnes"). This renunciation of the phallus, then, has the effect (side effect) of reinstating the phallus at an even higher level of transcendence. Parallel to this is Freud's later refusal to imagine a dephallicized masculinity as anything but castration. If we read this way, then the "racism" of the representation of the gentile male in European Jewish culture is more cultural critique than chauvinism. The diasporized male, as opposed to the politically dominant one, may have access to a different sense of his own sexuality.

Contrast with a medieval European text is illuminating here, namely Kathryn Gravdal's description of the Renart texts in medieval French: "The character of Hersent and the story of her rape by the hero open a space for a cynical parody that strips courtly discourse of its idealizing pretensions and scathingly mocks the feminizing ethos of romance" (1991, 74–75). Where Renart provides, however, cynical demystifications of a prevailing ideology, we suggest that the Talmudic text both avows and suspects its own cultural formation at one and the same time. The French text is openly parodic of its culture; the Talmudic text a more complicated representative of the official culture that it also interrogates. Late antique Jewish culture,[64] we suggest, rejects the phallus as a representation of male sexuality and thus imagines the possibility of a nonphallic male sexuality. We do not claim that it successfully achieves it. Remarkably, neither does the Talmud make that claim, as we shall see in the next section. In other words, we hypothesize here the Talmud as a resisting reader of itself.

Another narrative sequence, a rich and strange Talmudic legend of male desire and pain provides—perhaps in its most extreme Jewish (i.e., non-Christian) formulation—precisely the "inversion of aristocratic value equations" that Nietzsche so despised. The inversion is thematized in terms of gender reversals, or femminizations, explicitly in terms of the response of the politically weak Jews to the politically strong Romans.

Amy Richlin has made the interesting claim that "though the structure remains fixed, the identity of each position can change much more readily for imperialism than for gender: Etruria-owns-Rome becomes Rome-owns-Etruria, while the bottom position in a model for gender qua gender is female. In Rome, as in other imperialist cultures, an upper-class woman could own a male slave or far outrank a lower-class male; for class, as for empire, the bottom position would tend to be feminized" (1992, xviii). The question that needs to be asked, however, is: from whose point of view? Did those men "on the bottom" see themselves as feminized? And if and when they did, what was the value placed on feminization by those men? We can begin to suggest through studying early

Christian and Jewish texts at least a tentative and partial answer to this question, namely, that even for those men "on the bottom," being there was indeed interpreted as feminization, but feminization itself was transvalued and received at least some positive significance.

Cops and Rabbis

The text begins on a purely political note that seems hardly to have anything to do with gender:

> Rabbi El'azar the son of Rabbi Shim'on found a certain officer of the king who used to catch thieves. He [the Rabbi] asked him [the officer], "How do you prevail over them? Aren't they compared to animals, as it is written, 'at night tramp all the animals of the forest' (Psalms 104:20)?" *There are those who say that he said it to him from the following verse: "He will ambush from a hiding place like a lion in a thicket" (Psalms 10:9).* Said he to him, "Perhaps you are taking the innocent and leaving the guilty."
>
> He [the officer] said to him, "How shall I do it?"
>
> He [the Rabbi] said to him, "Come, I will teach you how to do it. Go in the first four hours of the morning to the wine bar. If you see someone drinking wine and falling asleep, ask of him what his profession is. If he is a rabbinical student, he has arisen early for study. If he is a day laborer, he has arisen early to his labor. If he worked at night, [find out if] perhaps it is metal smelting [a silent form of work], and if not, then he is a thief and seize him."
>
> The rumor reached the king's house, and he [the king] said, "Let him who read the proclamation be the one to execute it." They brought Rabbi El'azar the son of Rabbi Shim'on, and he began to catch thieves. He met Rabbi Yehoshua, the Bald, who said to him, "Vinegar son of Wine: how long will you persist in sending the people of our God to death?"
>
> He [Rabbi El'azar] said to him, "I am removing thorns from the vineyard."

He [Rabbi Yehoshua] said to him, "Let the Owner of the vineyard come and remove the thorns." (Baba Metsiaʿ 83b)

This brief story is about resistance to and collaboration with Roman domination. It thematizes, as well, blatant abuse of power. It is, therefore, a text that teaches us much about rabbinic ideologies of power and resistance. As we have seen, such ideologies are intimately involved with models of gender. The text assumes the subjugated status of the Jews to Roman rule, a status that strains the legitimacy of the internal leadership by the Rabbis of the Jewish polity. This text powerfully treats the question of diasporic modes of deceptive or trickster resistance versus martyrdom.

The story begins by assuming that thieves are necessarily stronger than those who seek to catch them. The rabbi cannot believe that the officer of the king is successfully catching thieves, since they are compared to animals, and on the physical plane it is understood that animals will always defeat human beings. Therefore his expression that "perhaps you are taking the innocent and leaving the guilty" is itself less than innocent, the "perhaps" only a bit of self-protection. He is saying that surely you are taking the innocent and leaving the guilty.

A certain orientation toward physicality is already being projected here. Thieves are analogized to animals, and animals are associated with strength. The opposite of this proposition would be that humans, i.e., being human, what later Judaism would call being a "mentsh," are precisely defined by physical weakness. The rabbi assumes that if the officer is indeed catching somebody, it must be innocent people, since otherwise how could he, a mentsh and weak, be successful against those who are bestial and strong? In other words, we suggest, the semiotics of this text at its very beginning sets up the paradigm of valorized weakness versus a denigrated physical strength. Moreover, the "text-critical" gloss that offers an alternative verse specifies precisely what the animal in question was, a lion. If the villains of the piece are compared to lions, the heroes must, of course, be the lambs.

This imagery, not only Christian, was continued throughout the Jewish Middle Ages. Thus we find, in a medieval Hebrew prayer for the atonement season, "*Through my guilt I am likened to and resemble a lion in the forest,* my utterance is foolish, my language is unintelligible! Faint, banished, and despised, I am shaken and tossed about. Drunken and intoxicated with wormwood, I am become full of sorrow and grief and oppressed by masters, to whom I was sold for naught; yet when my soul fainted within me, I remembered the Lord. I remembered thy kindness and love which were as a banner over me; they removed my guilt and made me thy treasure; *thy lambs now accustom themselves to prayers and entreaty,* the poorest among men exult in the Holy One of Israel" (Rosenfeld 1978). There is, of course, much to be said about this text and cognates that cannot be said here, but it is worth emphasizing that lionlike is clearly not what the speaker desires to be; being like a lion describes his guilt, while being a lamb is the attribute of his probity. It would not be entirely unwarranted to compare this text with the Sermon on the Mount.[65]

As in the previous section, in place of power, Rabbi El'azar (not the same one, but the coincidence in names is interesting) proposes stealth as a tool to defeat power. It is as if the text says neither the brute physical power of the animal-like thieves nor even the more rational and controlled power of the Roman government, but only cultural knowledge and cunning will prevail in the end. Since he has given this "good" advice, the rabbi has established that he sees the fate of the Jews as tied to the good order that the Romans can provide. He is accordingly recruited by the Roman authorities as a collaborator who turns over Jewish thieves to the Roman authorities.

This behavior is roundly condemned by the narrative. Another rabbinic voice within the text calls Rabbi El'azar "Vinegar son of Wine" (i.e., Wicked One, Son of a Saint) and asks, "How long will you persist in sending the people of our God to death?" Although the capture and punishment of thieves would normally be accepted practice, in a diasporic situation what appears as a judicial act is an act of treachery. Where the texts above thematized staying alive at all costs in order that the people and the Torah would continue, here we have the slip into collaboration that threatens the lives of the people, and the hero becomes villain. It is feigned collaboration as resistance that is valued as colonial ethic, not real collaboration. As long as the rabbi's advice to the Roman policeman consisted of techniques for preventing the capture of innocents, then his behavior was satisfactory, but as soon as he himself began to engage in capturing thieves—even guilty ones[66]—and turning them over to the Romans who would execute them, he was condemned.

The narrative goes on to elaborate further the consequences of collaboration or, rather, of deployment of physical political power:

> One day a certain laundry man met him and called him "Vinegar son of Wine." He said, "Since he is so brazen, one can assume that he is wicked." He said, "Seize him." They seized him. After he had settled down, he went in to release him, but he could not. He applied to him the verse, "One who guards his mouth and his tongue, guards himself from troubles" (Proverbs 21:23). They hung him. He stood under the hanged man and cried. Someone said to him, "Be not troubled; he and his son both had intercourse with an engaged girl on *Yom Kippur.*" In that minute, he placed his hands on his guts, and said, "Be joyful, O my guts, be joyful! If it is thus when you are doubtful, when you are certain even more so. I am confident that rot and worms cannot prevail over you."
>
> But even so, he was not calmed. They gave him a sleeping potion and took him into a marble room and ripped open his stomach and were taking out baskets of fat and placing it in

the July sun and it did not stink. He applied to himself the
verse, "even my flesh will remain preserved." (Psalms 16:8–9)

In a fit of anger, our hero uses his imperial (and imperious)
power to condemn to death a Jew who has opposed him. He
immediately, however, realizes what a terrible thing he has
done and tries to retrieve it, but cannot. Applying to himself
(or to the dead man) the verse from Proverbs regarding the terrible power of speech, he is desolate. Upon being reassured
that indeed the dead man eminently deserved death by Jewish
law, he at first affirms the value of his "gut" reaction but still
remains doubtful as to the righteousness of his own actions.
The rabbi performs a bizarre test on himself for righteousness.
In order to demonstrate that his actions with regard to the Jew
that he sent to his death were blameless ones, he attempts to
prove (to himself) that his body is indeed impermeable—i.e.,
that he possesses the "classical" phallic body, the body that, at
least since Plato, has always been associated *by male culture*
with the male, while the open, permeable, porous, embodied
body is "female."[67]

Here the different contradictory enactments of "male
envy" reveal their different political and ethical possibilities,
for a strategy that deals with male envy by denying value to
bodily creation and appropriating all creativity to thought
and political power is very different from one within which
men enact a desire for femaleness via the subversion of the
impermeability of their own bodies. In other words, the
rabbi's efforts to gain "the phallus" will be thematized as having directly opposite effects to his later ones to renounce the
phallus by mimesis of femaleness. Both are male strategies for
dealing with sexual difference and neither has much to do
with (or promise for) women, but, we insist, they nevertheless
have quite different political and ethical effects. As Pateman
has argued, classical liberal and statist feminism is grounded
in the argument that women have the same capabilities as
men (because classical patriarchal theory grounded itself in

the argument that they do not), but "struggle over this terrain presupposes that there is no political significance in the fact that women have an ability that men lack" (95). In other words, rather than an acknowledgement of male envy of female ability, "the phallus" and all of the political theory that it entails is a massive mystification and disavowal of that envy. Without claiming any utopian (or even protofeminist) moment for rabbinic and early Christian culture through this analysis, we would nevertheless suggest that the challenge to the phallic, classical body that texts such as ours enact (however—or because it is—riddled with self-contradiction) provides an Archimedean point for critique, another of the potential powers of diaspora.

Our "hero" problematizes the phallic understanding of masculinity paradoxically through his own attempts to substantiate it. He begins by making the claim that since he is so certain that he is righteous, he is equally sure that his body will be impervious to the depredations of worms after his death. That is, he imagines himself as the classic impermeable body, the body that is pristine and closed off from the outside world—"even my flesh will remain preserved." Ironically, however, the test that the rabbi devises in order to prove his self-image is precisely one that undermines it. He has the integrity of his body violated in the bizarre operation of removing basketfuls of fat from his stomach and having them placed in the sun to see if they will, indeed, be immune from rotting. We have then an incredible moment of self-destruction of the very models of masculinity that are being both proposed and defeated at the same time.

As Mikhail Bakhtin has pointed out, the image of the body part grown out of all proportion is "actually a picture of dismemberment, of separate areas of the body enlarged to gigantic dimensions" (1984, 328). The rabbi is clearly grotesquely obese if several basketfuls of fat could be removed from his body. The topoi of exaggerated size, detachable organs, the emphasis on the orifices and stories of dismemberment are all representations of the body as interacting with the world, not self-enclosed as the classical body. Moreover, the association of the coherent, impermeable body with imperial power is thematized directly in the story as well. When the rabbi acted in consonance with imperial power, he was attacked by the text. However, when the rabbi allows his body to be dismembered, to be grotesquified, in a process that is almost parodic of birth as well as castration, then he is validated by the text.[68] The Talmudic text bears out Bakhtin's remarkable insight by combining in one moment the monstrous belly that "hides the normal members of the body" and the actual dismemberment of that monstrous organ. Indeed, the image of what is done to the body of the rabbi is almost a mad Caesarean section, a parodic appropriation of female fecundity. In other words, this operation is a form of critique of male power through a mimesis of femaleness. The logic of referring to it as appropriation grows out of the very fact that it uses the female body as its metaphor for critique of modes of male hegemony. We do not discount the critique of male power or its usefulness if, at the same time, we pay skeptical attention to the fact that it "shifts the gaze away from the physical suffering of the female body to the dilemmas of men" (Gravdal 1991, 15).

If we imaginatively think through what it was that this rabbi was feeling guilty for, namely, collaboration with the violence of the Roman authorities, then this particular response, grotesquifying and femminizing his body, makes perfect sense. If the violence of Rome was experienced as a peculiarly male imposition, then correction of having participated in this violence would require a self-femminization. This representation, the necessity to become female in order to renounce and repent for violence, is iterated within the Talmudic text at several junctures. This response, moreover, has positive meanings as well—and not only corrective or reactive ones—just as and just because the grotesque body itself is suffused with creative power: "All these convexities and orifices have a common characteristic; it is within them that the con-

fines between bodies and between the body and the world are
overcome: there is an interchange and an interorientation"
(Bakhtin 1984, 317). This body can be taken, then, as an
ideal representation of Jewish culture in diaspora as a site
where the confines between the body of Jewish culture and
other social bodies are overcome,[69] not forgetting, of course,
the frequently violent response from many of those other
bodies. Paradoxically, however, this diasporization of the
body is also a pursuit of purity, of a moral pristineness that
engagement with power seemingly would preclude. This paradox of diaspora as the site of purity and cultural interchange
is inherent in postbiblical Jewish culture, as we have seen in
the first part of this chapter. No wonder then that the rabbi's
body is both purified and violated in the same operation,
rendered classical through precisely that which marks it as
grotesque.

The dismembered, "castrated" male body is also deterrito-
rialized, as the text troubles to relate to us in its continuation.
Another of the rabbis, put into precisely the same situation of
either collaboration with Roman tyranny or probably dangerous resistance, is urged to simply run away:

> To Rabbi Ishmaʿel the son of Yose there also occurred a simi-
> lar situation. Eliahu (the Prophet Elijah) met him and said to
> him, "How long will you persist in sending the people of our
> God to death?" He said to him, "What can I do; it is the king's
> order?" He said to him, "Your father ran away to Asia Minor;
> you run away to Lydia."

The appropriate form of resistance that the Talmud recommends for Jews in this place is evasion. The arts of colonized peoples of dissimulation and dodging are thematized
here as actually running away, the very opposite of such
"masculine" pursuits as "standing one's ground." Above, we
have encountered the myth of the foundation of rabbinic Judaism in such an act of evasion and trickery, the "grotesque"
escape of Rabbi Yoḥanan ben Zakkai from besieged Jerusalem

in a coffin, which the rabbis portray as the very antithesis of the military resistance of the Zealots who wanted to fight to the very last man and preserve their honor. Here we find the same political theory—"Get out of there!"—adumbrated in a much less direct and richer way. The text designates diasporic modes of resistance, deterritorialization, and the grotesque, dismembered, dephallicized male body; resistance not as the accession to power and dominance, but as resistance *to* the assumption of dominance: "run away to Lydia," and this prescription is put into the mouth of one of the most authoritative oracles that rabbinic culture can produce, Elijah the Prophet. Nor is this recommendation unique in rabbinic texts. As the Palestinian Talmud recommends, "If they propose that you be a member of the *boule*,[70] let the Jordan be your border" (Mo'ed Katan 2:3, 81b; Sanhedrin 8:2, 26b). The tenacity that is valorized by these texts is the tenacity that enables continued Jewish existence, not the tenacity of defending sovereignty unto death.

Circumscribing Constitutional Identities in *Kiryas Joel*

Circumscribing Constitutional
Identities in *Kiryas Joel*

The *Kiryas Joel* case decided by the U.S. Supreme Court in
1994 turned on the constitutionality, under the Establishment
Clause of the First Amendment, of New York State legislation
establishing a separate school district providing special education exclusively for Hasidic Jewish children.[1] That legislation was deemed to be an unconstitutional establishment of
religion. However, in line with certain dicta of the Court, the
legislation was redrafted in a fashion that appeared to permit
the separate school district to continue in existence. At present the fate of the district is once again being litigated.

A substantial amount of commentary has already been
written about *Kiryas Joel*. So-called student notes on the case
in law journals are frequently concerned with the implications of *Kiryas Joel* for Supreme Court standards in deciding
religious establishment cases—an area of law that has been
notoriously troublesome to the Court in recent decades (e.g.,
Acklin 1995; Thomas 1994). Professors have analyzed the
case as an example of the current Court's secularist bias (Berg
1995) and as exemplifying the need to examine constitutional
issues from the perspective of minority groups (Minow 1995,

"Constitution"). The most exhaustive exchange on *Kiryas Joel* is anchored by an article by Professor Abner Greene (1996), who argues strongly for the right to semiautonomy of groups that demonstrate their commitment to their own principles by separating themselves geographically. Accompanying Greene's article are responses by Christopher Eisgruber, who claims that assimilation is a constitutional value (1996), and by Ira Lupu, who is concerned that the current arrangement masks abuses of democratic process within Kiryas Joel (1996).

What has not been pointed out is that the judicial opinions and the legal commentary on *Kiryas Joel* share a common underlying conception of the relation between identity (the nature of the subject of rights) and polity (the constituency of the state). In that underlying conception, the polity is understood as consisting of all the citizens of a neutrally bounded territory (a municipality or state), while the subject of rights is taken to be the individual person. These assumptions of neutral territory and the individual subject shape all of the previous literature on *Kiryas Joel*, which has not acknowledged an alternative underlying conception of political identity as organized around diaspora (primary orientation elsewhere than a group's present residence) and genealogy (family and group descent and upbringing). This alternative underlying conception animates the residents of Kiryas Joel in their search for culturally acceptable provision of special education.

The Place and the Case

The residents of the Village of Kiryas Joel in New York State are known as Satmar Hasidim. Their lifestyle and social organization are devoted to observance of their understanding of the Torah, rabbinic teachings, and their ancestral communal traditions. They identify with other groups of Satmar Hasidim in the United States, Europe, and Israel, with related (and generally smaller) Hasidic communities, with all Orthodox Jews, and to a lesser extent perhaps, with all persons whom they regard as Jewish by birth. Their commitment to communal solidarity and their pragmatic relation to the surrounding population occasion conflicts both within the Satmar Hasidic community and beyond its communal boundaries.

After World War II, Joel Teitelbaum, known as the Satmarer Rov or Rebbe,[2] settled in the Williamsburg section of Brooklyn, New York. He was a dynamic and charismatic leader who managed to reconstitute a community of Satmar Hasidim. Over the decades following World War II, Williamsburg became a thriving center of Hasidic life, containing numerous Hasidic groups in close proximity to each other. As communities were reassembled and the survivors' families multiplied, that area of Williamsburg readily available to Hasidic residents became extremely crowded. This fostered the establishment of various "satellite" communities in upstate New York, while Williamsburg remains a lively Hasidic neighborhood.

One such satellite was established by Satmar Hasidim in an area of Monroe, New York. Several years later a zoning dispute arose, leading to the establishment in 1977 of the separate Village of Kiryas Joel. The new village was comprised exclusively of Satmar Hasidim, substantially because neighbors who did not want to secede with the Satmars objected.

Because of the universal preference for private religious schooling among the Satmar Hasidim in Kiryas Joel, particular arrangements have been made for the provision of publicly funded special education services to handicapped Satmar children there. For one year beginning in 1984, such services were provided by the Monroe-Woodbury School District at an annex to the Bais Rochel girls school, but this arrangement was ended after the Supreme Court decisions in *Grand Rapids v. Ball*[3] and *Aguilar v. Felton*.[4] Instead, the Monroe-Woodbury district offered special education for the Satmar children in regular public schools, which their families found highly unsatisfactory. Ultimately the New York legislature passed the statute challenged by the litigation in this case, specifically naming the Village of Kiryas Joel as an independent school district with plenary powers. Special education services have subsequently been provided to Hasidic children from Kiryas Joel as well as neighboring districts. The head of the special education school—the only school, in fact, that is run by the Kirgas Joel school district—is not Jewish, and the school's curriculum is thoroughly secular. Not all the residents of the village support this arrangement for the education of Kiryas Joel's handicapped children.

Justice Souter announced the judgment of the Court. The bulk of his opinion was joined by four other justices, and another part by only three of his fellows. There were three separate concurring opinions, by Justices Stevens, Kennedy, and O'Connor. Justice Scalia filed a dissent, joined by Chief Justice Rehnquist and Justice Thomas. Finding anomalous the creation of the smaller school district when the general trend was toward consolidation, and concerned that the residents of Kiryas Joel had benefited from a special act of the legislature, the Court found the legislation establishing the district to be an unconstitutional establishment of religion. Justice O'Connor's concurrence, however, suggested that government action accomplishing the same end but "implemented through generally acceptable legislation" would be acceptable. Promptly following the announcement, the New York legislature redrafted the legislation in more general terms.[5] The new legislation was challenged in turn. In August 1996 the Appellate Division of the New York Supreme Court ruled the new legislation unconstitutional, finding that rather than "set[ting] forth neutral criteria that a village must meet to have a school district of its own, . . . in enacting the current law, the Legislature simply resurrected the prior law by achieving exactly the same result through carefully crafted indirect means."[6]

Frames of Juridical Identity

The notion of identity implicit in U.S. constitutionalist discourse relies on two interlinked principles. The first of these is the normativity of Protestant individualism in all its denominational variety.[7] The notion of religious freedoms—*from* the coercion of state religion and *to* exercise religion—contemplated by the drafters of the First Amendment doubtless reflected the Protestant emphasis on individual faith as the bedrock of religious integrity. Faith and individualism both facilitated the separation of a public sphere substantially shaped by state law from a more autonomous private sphere.[8]

The second of the two interlinked principles is "the long-standing Anglo-American commitment to organizing political representation around geography."[9] Governments and their constituencies are thus bounded by geographic lines. This commitment is so deeply ingrained in our normative political culture that it is often difficult to see how representation could be conceived otherwise.[10] As the political philosopher William Connolly explains, "The democratic, territorial state sets itself up to be the sovereign protector of its people, the highest site of their allegiance, and the organizational basis of their nationhood" (1995).[11] However, "few states, if any, actually maintain close alignment between this image of the sovereign, territorial, national, democratic security state and their actual practices" (136). In actuality all states are riven by failures to guarantee personal security and democratic freedoms, by hierarchizing myths that systematically exclude certain categories of persons from full participation within the presumed national collective, and by the existence of profound competing loyalties among their constituents. Given especially this last gap between state ideal and state practice, it is no surprise that constitutional debates frequently turn on the degree of accommodation the state will make to the "actual practices" of its citizens.

Litigation strategies may reflect implicit awareness of individualist and/or territorial conceptions of identity. Thus one of the signal ironies of *Kiryas Joel* is the reflection of individualist bias in the court papers on behalf of the school district. "The Satmar[12] did not claim that separation from non-Satmar was religiously required, explaining that they live together and avoid integration with the larger community 'to facilitate *individual* religious observance and maintain social, cultural and religious values.'"[13] This stance on the part of the legal representatives of the Kiryas Joel residents is cast in the terms of a value-neutral, territorial choice. It seems designed on the one hand to avoid any overtones of the kind of segregation discouraged in racial discrimination cases, and on the other hand to emphasize the individual subject of the right to religious freedoms.[14] It is true that when the Village of Kiryas Joel was originally set up, the village boundary lines were drawn "so as to exclude all but Satmars."[15] The record suggests, however, that this was largely because those neighbors who were not Satmar Hasidim did not want to be in the secessionist village.

The extent to which the dossier on *Kiryas Joel* assumes that the particular values and collective understandings—the "nomos"—of the residents of Kiryas Joel are relevant to the case points to the influence of Robert Cover's classic essay "Nomos and Narrative" (1983), published a decade before the *Kiryas Joel* litigation was moving through the courts. "Nomos and Narrative" is relevant because *Kiryas Joel* throws into question the individualist and territorial assumptions underlying the ideal of an objective, rule-based body of law, an ideal that Cover's critique eloquently undermines in turn. "Nomos and Narrative" challenges a purely formal or proceduralist conception of liberal state jurisprudence. Cover in effect denies that any judgment can be made on the basis of purely objective, universally valid legal principles. Rather, he asserts that the state should take seriously self-governing communities' claims to interpret the Constitution as it applies to them.

The essay begins with the announcement that "[w]e inhabit a nomos—a normative universe" (4). This "normative universe is held together by the force of interpretive commitments—some small and private, others immense and public" (7). Those interpretive commitments are contained in "narratives in which the corpus juris is located" (9) and thus determine the meaning of law. "Nomos and Narrative" thus presents a theory of tensions within constitutional jurisprudence that makes strong claims for the jurisprudential authority of largely self-governing communities such as the Hasidic community of Kiryas Joel.[16]

Furthermore, "Nomos and Narrative" centers on a case, *Bob Jones University*,[17] which has been cited by at least one authority as presenting issues analogous to those in *Kiryas Joel* (Lupu 1996). *Bob Jones* was not the easiest test of Cover's thesis that the claims of self-governing communities should be taken seriously vis-à-vis the "imperial" state. In that case, Bob Jones University claimed the right to maintain tax-exempt status and also the right to practice racial exclusion in its admissions process. Cover, who had participated in the twentieth-century fight for civil rights, would hardly have shared the University's value of white separatism. In this light the nomos in *Bob Jones* appears unattractive in comparison to the imperial lawmaking authority of the democratic state. That the argument for "taking nomoi seriously," so to speak, could be made by taking such an unattractive nomos as exemplary adds continuing resonance to Cover's argument. Nevertheless, many commentators recognize *Kiryas Joel* as an even more poetically appropriate test of Cover's argument in "Nomos and Narrative."[18]

Yet *Kiryas Joel* actually points toward flawed or incomplete points in "Nomos and Narrative." First, one of the major foci there is the concept of "jurisgeneration," by which Cover means the creative aspect of jurisprudence, the "principle by which legal meaning proliferates in all communities" (11). That creative process is largely contained in narratives that the juridical community tells to itself. For Cover, jurisgeneration seems to be the province of authoritative adult males creating law through discourse. Nowhere in "Nomos and Narrative" does Cover relate meaning-creating narratives to generation in its more immediate sense—to the biocultural reproduction of groups owing allegiance to their own nomoi. That form of generation or genealogy, as we argue below, is crucial to understanding the situation of the people of the Village of Kiryas Joel.[19] Without it, Cover's focus on covenantal communities reinforces a tendency to misunderstand the Kiryas Joel community by analogy to groups of Protestant dissidents.

Second, Cover's eloquent account of the interpretive and meaning-producing claims of small-scale communities facing the liberal state casts these as claims about interpretation of the U.S. Constitution. Thus, discussing the rights of Mennonite religious communities, he asserts, "I am making a very strong claim for the Mennonite understanding of the first amendment" (28). He does not address the possibility that communal self-understandings (such as those we call diasporic) may ignore, rather than contest or seek to conform to, the broader jurisprudential nomos of the state. This helps enable a claim that *only* those communal understandings that overtly contest and hence invigorate the majority consensus are worthy of any constitutional deference. Cover's broad arguments about the relation between meaning-generating communities and the conflicts of individual and group rights can and should be invigorated with regard to *Kiryas Joel* through the concepts of genealogy and diaspora.

As contemporary language theory asserts, metaphors and narratives are not mere ornamentations, but central to the construction of meaning in and through language (Lakoff and Johnson 1980; White 1981). We will therefore miss important aspects of the literature surrounding *Kiryas Joel* unless we attend to the way the story is told, the social categories into which the residents are placed, and the images employed in descriptions of the conflict. In *Kiryas Joel,* much turns on the actual political implications of territorial boundaries presumed to be neutral. Hence analyses of *Kiryas Joel* frequently involve recourse to spatial metaphors and narrative models that help structure our conceptions of the issues involved.

Constitutional debates about religion are often cast against the legendary background of the Puritan colonists in North America. The Protestant founding communities explicitly understood themselves as analogous to Israelites, and thus as being in a "covenantal" relationship vis-à-vis God and each other (Levinson 1988). It is easy to connect the Jewish Satmar group as a further link in this chain of covenantal communities, and there are numerous reasons why it is tempting to assimilate the residents of Kiryas Joel to the Pilgrim migrants to America. The move of a segment of the Satmar Hasidic community from Williamsburg, Brooklyn, to upstate New York is sometimes referred to as an "exodus" (Olivo 1993, 775–817). There is a mixture of evocations here, between leaving Babylon (the city) and leaving Egypt for the promised land of Monroe.

Such an association, even if implicit, lends credibility to Abner Greene's notions of complete exit (exemplified by the *Yoder* case that established the right of Amish parents to keep children out of school) and partial exit (as in *Kiryas Joel*) as legitimate grounds for communal autonomy. At least one commentator has made the further, and clearly erroneous, association between Satmar Hasidim and Protestant groups on the basis of biblical literalism.[20] The connection that makes this a peculiarly American exodus, however, is the evocation of the Protestant errand into the wilderness in search of a place to be faithful and pure (Miller 1956). The model for such an exodus within the American continent would in turn be Roger Williams, who left to found a new religious/political/geographic community made up of people who shared his dissident faith (Smith 1995).

Martha Minow uses a different spatial metaphor to illustrate why *Yoder* is perhaps a less "hard case" than *Kiryas Joel.* She argues that the claims to the right to be left alone made by the Amish parents are congenial with the terms of the Constitution. Thus for Minow the situation in *Yoder* "supports an image of Russian nesting dolls in which each subcommunity fits comfortably within the larger enclosure of the dominant state" (Minow 1995, "Rights and Cultural Differences," 357). *Kiryas Joel*, in Minow's view, represents a conflictual model illustrated by "an image of spinning tops, each pursuing its own orbit but occasionally running into another, with such collisions setting each off balance."

Yet another spatial metaphor is employed by Nomi Stolzenberg. Drawing on Emily Dickinson's poem "He Drew a Circle That Shut Me Out," Stolzenberg employs a dynamic metaphor of inclusive and exclusive circles. At the center of such imaginary circles are the members of either larger and usually dominant or smaller and often subordinate groups—e.g., "the people of Monroe" or "the Satmar Hasidim." In some situations the circles are drawn large, to include even those who do not share the identity at the center of the circle. In other situations they are drawn narrowly, to circumscribe the core group. When they are large, they can be tolerant ("feel free to join us") or coercive ("you must become like us"). When small, they may be protective ("leave us to ourselves") or, again, coercive ("you may not go outside") (1993, 585).

The more nuanced view of group relations suggested by these spatial metaphors casts in a new light the insistence in the school district brief that mixing with nonreligious children was not "against the religion" of the Satmar Hasidim. Nothing in biblical or rabbinic law mandates total segregation from non-Jews. Yet various Jewish laws, maxims, and customs have been deployed since biblical times to enforce the cultural boundaries of the group, to the extent that an effort to minimize contact with non-Jewish culture could plausibly be claimed as a religious mandate. Had the case been defended on free exercise grounds, the claim for such a religious mandate might have been sound strategy.[21] The failure to make such a claim might have resulted from the school board's primary concern to fend off an adverse ruling based on the Establishment Clause. If so, this would also explain their insistence on the children's being upset in the public schools as the full reason why they were asking for legislative action to allow separate but public schools for handicapped children. If such considerations of litigation strategy forced a significant distortion of their collective self-representation, it may be that notions of spatial equilibrium (tension, balance, or neutrality) between the Establishment Clause and the Free Exercise Clause of the First Amendment are actually harmful to effective jurisprudence.[22] Such judicial objective equilibrium is in any case an impossibility.[23] In cases like *Yoder* and *Kiryas Joel,* a court will always have to draw the circle somewhere.

Sect, Subgroup, and Subcommunity

In a broad sense the opinions and surrounding legal discussions of *Kiryas Joel are* the case. As we will discuss later, a good deal of the judicial and scholarly discussion of the case hinges on the putative neutrality of the criteria by which the village and school district were established. Examination of the putatively neutral categories used to describe the Kiryas Joel Satmar as a group reveals how the seemingly neutral terms "sect," "subgroup," and "subcommunity" betray an assumption that citizens should identify primarily as "individual Americans."

Justice Souter's opinion begins quite carefully, merely referring to the Satmar Hasidim as "practitioners of a strict form of Judaism."[24] Later in the opinion, however, he refers to them as a "sect." This terminology is echoed in the various student notes on *Kiryas Joel* and on *Grumet.*[25] Why this term should seem apt is not immediately evident. Its definition in the *American Heritage Dictionary* emphasizes distinctness within a larger group, religious character, and shared interests or beliefs, and traces the term to the Latin *secta,* "course, school of thought." *Roget's Thesaurus* confirms the intellectual and religious emphases of the term. Both of these definitions rely on the notion of a religious group as a set of otherwise autonomous individuals coming together in shared faith. Nothing in them suggests the likelihood of kinship bonds among members of sects. Nothing about "subgroup," "subcommunity," or "sect" adequately suggests the genealogical ties that are crucial to maintaining a diasporic communal nomos.[26]

The title of Martha Minow's essay, "The Constitution and the Subgroup Question" (1995) suggests her intention to place the case in the context of Jewish "minority" status. As her prefatory thumbnail sketch of Jewish history suggests, Jews seem to be a sort of paradigm "subgroup" for her, and she states her title is meant "to allude . . . to the phrase 'the Jewish question'" (1). More generally, the primary group with respect to whom the residents of Kiryas Joel might appear as a subgroup in Minow's account are "Americans"— that group constituted by the Constitution. Minow's phrase is troubling, for in marking only the "subgroup" for question, it may leave the impression that this larger group may be taken for granted as sharing a normative identity that makes them American. If the group is "Americans" and subgroups are subject to question, are they part of the group or not? The use of the term "subgroup" effectively undermines Minow's stated goal of explaining the background to *Kiryas Joel* from the subgroup's own perspective.

Christopher Eisgruber, responding to Abner Greene's essay in defense of the right to partial exit, relies on a claim of American collective identity as a positive social phenomenon that the Constitution is designed to foster. Because he believes that collective identity is sustained in part by challenges to its own self-justification, he finds that the Constitution has a place for what he calls "sub-communities." The place normative constitutionalism grants to subcommunities is, in Eisgruber's view, therefore dependent on those subcommunities' ability to provoke reflective self-questioning within the constitutional polity: "because reflective constitutionalism is self-critical about the good, it values such sub-communities as sources of dissent and respects them as sincere efforts to pursue a vision of the good that might, after all, prove correct" (1996, 91). Eisgruber thus forces all distinctive groups into the model of principled dissenters. This is particularly unfortunate for the evaluation of the Satmar Hasidim. They are more interested in carrying out a contract that they believe their ancestors made with God than in promoting the universal correctness of their "vision of the good." Given Eisgruber's criteria, it is not clear why the United States should accommodate groups that "like the Satmars and the Amish, reject[] principles of justice fundamental to the American regime."

Ira Lupu employs the notion of subcommunities as well, but questions whether such subcommunities are really governed by the integrity of an internal nomos. Unlike Eisgruber's by now more conventional association of the Satmar Hasidim and the Amish, Lupu analogizes Kiryas Joel not only to Bob Jones University, but to much more ominous names in the news. Thus Lupu claims that Abner Greene's analysis of varieties of social evil is not helpful with regard to "the sort of problems presented by *Kiryas Joel, Bob Jones University,* the Waco Branch Davidians, the Montana Militia, and the myriad sub-communities to which it might be applied" (1996, 110). Here "subcommunity" acquires some of the same negative connotations as "sect."

The ominous connotations of sectarianism[27] and the actuality of bitter struggles within Kiryas Joel are at the heart of Lupu's "Uncovering the Village of Kiryas Joel." Lupu argues that "the structure of authority in the Village presented an unusually high risk of unconstitutional governance. So uncovered, the Village appears to be a poor candidate for the dual rule of nomic community and repository of state power" (104–5). Lupu means to demystify the idea of the Satmar nomos. His title thus represents a complex pun. At one level it has an aggressively investigative connotation. Lupu purports to dig beneath the surface of the official court representation of the issues, bringing in the "dirt" about the heart of darkness constituting Kiryas Joel's undemocratic structure. Lupu also aims to dispel Justice Scalia's suggestion that it is ludicrous to think of the Satmar Hasidim as enjoying anything like the degree of power that could make them likely candidates for the establishment of religion.[28] Responding to Scalia, Lupu stresses that Hasidic Jews are a well-organized "non-ideological swing vote group," well-connected to the administration of Governor Mario Cuomo.[29] Ultimately, Lupu aims to demystify the more romantic readings of Cover's original idea of nomic communities. Thus Lupu suspects "that so-called nomic communities are likely to reveal a high frequency of constitution-flouting."[30]

Doubtless he is correct on this point. Cover himself acknowledged that Jewish communities in diaspora have perpetuated themselves partly through the deployment of forms of coercion, albeit forms short of the state power for which he reserved the term "violence" (1983). Speculations about the frequency of Constitution flouting should not determine the constitutionality of granting different governmental powers to different kinds of communities. Actual violations of voting rights or free speech should be dealt with by ordinary police powers. This is the mechanism dictated by the balance in the United States between state police powers and the range of relations between politics and identities.[31] If metaphors constitute meaningful language, we must be careful of the metaphors we use. Here at least the "uncovering" pun has led Lupu's jurisprudence astray.

The emphasis on metaphors and categories is not meant to suggest that such terms and phrases uniquely or ultimately *determine* judicial or scholarly opinions. They range widely from overt suspicion of the Kiryas Joel setup to frank sympathy for the right to be different. Yet all of them cast the Kiryas Joel community in some sort of "sub," secondary status vis-à-vis the normative group putatively governed by and faithful to the Constitution. "Sect," even where it is not pejorative, focuses on the feature of individual belief and occludes the genealogical dynamic, while "subgroup" and "subcommunity" imply outsider status. Whether to keep them out or pull them in, these categories draw subtly coercive circles.

Different Establishments

The relation between the establishment of the village and of the school district is discussed in Justice Souter's opinion for the Court. Souter distinguishes the creation of the Kiryas Joel district from two related and permissible processes. On the one hand, "[t]he district in this case is distinguishable from one whose boundaries are derived according to neutral historical and geographic criteria, but whose population happens to comprise coreligionists." On the other, the creation of the district "contrasts with the process by which the Village of Kiryas Joel was created, involving as it did, the application of a neutral state law designed to give almost any group of residents the right to incorporate."[32] These two statements appear to contradict one another. If the village was created in accord with a "neutral state law," and the school district conforms to the boundaries of the village, how do the boundaries of the district differ from "boundaries . . . derived according to . . . neutral criteria?" To see how this contradiction could pass unnoticed in Justice Souter's opinion, we must look more carefully at the implicit concepts governing the different views of the establishment of the village and of the school district.

Individual and territorial notions of the relation between space and identity are at the base of the *amici* briefs filed against the school district by several liberal Jewish oganizations. It is generally understood that such organizations pursue a legal agenda of the strictest separation of church and state on the premise that any weakening of the constitutional ban against religious establishments, even in favor of a minority group, is likely to inure sooner or later to the general detriment of religious minorities. These organizations may also have been less sympathetic to the Satmar Hasidim in general because of the Satmars' reputation for standoffishness vis-à-vis other Jews.[33] Remembering that these Jewish organizations argued against the village should make us wary of claims that the Court evidences "hostility" toward religion in general (see, e.g., Acklin 1995, 49).

The liberal Jewish organizations, like everyone else, jumped on the bandwagon too late. For those concerned with religious establishment, the litigation over the special school district in *Kiryas Joel* really should have followed litigation over the establishment of the village.[34] As Richard Ford has recently suggested, local municipal lines and school districts should be held to the same standard of constitutional scrutiny: "[I]f the states are not free to establish a system of segregated schools, they should not be allowed to accomplish the same objective by delegating state power to segregated localities" (1994, 1865).[35] The problems inherent in the establishment of the Village of Kiryas Joel were politically invisible because of our political culture's habitual failure to consider local space as a politically contingent issue, rather than as a given fact.

It is true that the primary motivation for the original establishment of the separate Village of Kiryas Joel in 1979 rested on nothing so lofty as desire for a pure and separate existence. Rather the issues were quite mundane, centering on taxation, concentration of extended families in areas with single-family zoning, and the proximity of houses of worship to residential areas.[36] These issues are not inherent to any religious separatism, but do have much to do with genealogy, given the tendency of Hasidic families to live in multigenerational households and to have numerous children per married couple. The practice of holding prayer services *in* houses (and the taxation disputes that may arise therefrom) likewise demonstrate the actual inseparability of "religion" from genealogy and ethnicity for a group like the Satmar Hasidim.

These mundane issues show that, while spatial metaphors may be powerful ways of talking about identity, space is more than just a metaphor. Diaspora is not a nonspatial existence, but a concrete relation between genealogy and space. Ironically, the residents of Kiryas Joel seceded because their land-use patterns were those that, in the general secession case, we would expect a group to secede in order to *avoid*—land-use patterns engaged in by poor people and their lower ratio of tax input to service demands (Ford 1994, 1870).

Thus, it is not simply "religious" separation that is at issue here. However, this point does not necessarily confirm Justice Scalia's argument that the creation of the village constituted "a classic drawing of lines on the basis of communality of *secular governmental desires*."[37] The mundane issues do not necessarily imply the absence of concerns we would commonly designate as religious. Ford's diagnosis of the blind spots in constitutional jurisprudence and scholarship stemming from our common naturalization of territory and geography suggest that, here, reading back from the fact that there *was* a village leads to the presumption that its foundation must have had a religiously neutral, "secular" basis. True, unlike the school district, the village "boundaries were established pursuant to a neutral, generally applicable state law, not through a special act of religious accommodation."[38] Again, however, the relative ease by which a municipality can be established suggests a low level of concern for the differential political impact on different groups of citizens of the redrawing of local political boundaries.[39]

One of the complicating aspects of *Kiryas Joel* is that religious establishment and equal-protection jurisprudence issues appear to be closely intertwined in the case. The vocabulary of judges and constitutional scholars lacks a concept like that of genealogy. Thus the separation of the Hasidic school children inevitably comes to be seen as analogous to an acceptable or unacceptable form of racial segregation.

Justice Kennedy draws on the legacy of equal protection decisions in distinguishing between the creation of the village and that of the school district, according to an implicit criterion of state action.[40] He describes the process by which "voluntary association . . . leads to a political community comprised of people who share a common religious faith." He contrasts this to the enactment of state legislation having the same result: "government may not use religion as a criterion to draw political or electoral lines. . . . In this respect, the Establishment Clause mirrors the Equal Protection Clause" (Walzer 1983).[41] The analogy as used by Kennedy is somewhat misleading. In equal protection cases, the line is not drawn between voluntary and governmental actions, but between private and state actions. The creation of the Kiryas Joel School District, while pursuant to a governmental action, nevertheless conformed to the will of the majority of Kiryas Joel residents.[42]

Equal protection analogies are also at the heart of Abner Greene's argument for the constitutionality of the Kiryas Joel arrangement. Greene suggests that *Kiryas Joel* is consistent with the fact pattern ruled on by the Supreme Court in *Keyes v. School District No. 1*[43] and *Milliken v. Bradley*: "if private citizens move to relatively homogeneous neighborhoods, government is not required to draw school attendance zones across neighborhoods."[44] However, in his very next sentence Greene quotes the Court's statement in *Keyes* that the distinction between impermissible de jure and permissible de facto segregation is "*purpose* or *intent* to segregate." It is by no means clear that the racial divisions across municipal boundaries that were at the base of the litigation in *Milliken,* for example, should properly have passed this "intent" test. Territory and geography should not be presumed to be socially neutral or "noninvidious." In any case, even if separation is not an essential tenet of Satmar beliefs, *Kiryas Joel* would fail the "intent" test, since the desire to maintain an integral community clearly underlies the series of legal maneuvers involved.

We have seen that supposedly neutral territorial divisions are actually rife with political significance. The question of the establishment of the Village of Kiryas Joel is not divorced from the constitutional question of the establishment of the school district. At the same time, distinguishing genealogy as a strategy of cultural maintenance from the racialist discrimination known in U.S. history suggests that the district should not be defended on the basis of decisions such as *Keyes* and *Milliken,* nor should the district be suspect by analogy to racial segregation. At this point, we finally reach the question of the well-being of the children who receive special education in Kiryas Joel.

Whatever segregation obtains between the municipalities of Kiryas Joel and Monroe, and between the school districts of Kiryas Joel and Monroe-Woodbury, is not solely the result of the voluntary political withdrawal of the residents of Kiryas Joel. Thomas Berg correctly notes that after the mid-1980s Supreme Court decisions in *Aguilar* and *Ball* cast in doubt the arrangement whereby special education services had been provided at public expense but at Kiryas Joel religious schools,

> The [Monroe-Woodbury] district then turned recalcitrant. It refused to offer classes elsewhere in the village, even though the Supreme Court had approved such programs at "a neutral site off the premises of [religious] schools," and instead required the Kiryas Joel children to come into the public schools for their tutoring. (1995, 436–37)

Eisgruber also notes that this option was available to the Monroe-Woodbury School District, but then goes on immediately to claim that it was "[t]he Kiryas Joel school district [sic] [that] refused to offer such classes" (1996, 93).[45] Indeed, Berg is almost alone among commentators in mentioning the "recalcitrance" of the Monroe-Woodbury district in his narrative of the case.

The recalcitrance of the Monroe-Woodbury administrators lends credence to the claim on behalf of Kiryas Joel that, when the handicapped students of Kiryas Joel were forced to attend special education classes in Monroe-Woodbury public schools, they suffered "panic, fear and trauma . . . in leaving their own community and being with people whose ways were so different."[46] Generally, the legal commentaries, regardless of their ultimate stance on the constitutionality of the district, accept at face value the Kiryas Joel residents' claim that the unfeasibility of having Hasidic handicapped children attend class with public school children was attendant on such outside discrimination.[47]

The stated objections to sending the Kiryas Joel handicapped children to Monroe-Woodbury public schools thus emphasize the external barriers faced by those children; in Stolzenberg's formulation, these barriers were "the circle that shut [the children] out." Evidently this was consistent with the village's strategy of de-emphasizing separatism as a Satmar tenet. It is difficult to believe, however, that the Satmar parents did not *want* to keep the children in the community. Indeed, it cannot be stressed enough how these children's "specialness" places them "at the mercy" of the Satmar community, the state, and public school officials. Attention to the needs of handicapped children, rather than a general tendency to hide them as an embarrassment and a potential bar to the marriage possibilities of other family members, is a relatively recent phenomenon in Hasidic communities (Mintz 1992). Handicaps are a stigma in society at large. If anything, they are an even greater stigma in communities obsessed with genealogy and everything that genealogy represents: the possibility of improving social standing through strategic links of extended families in marriage; the "quality" of a given person's ancestry as a valid aspect of that person's own value; the imperative to be fruitful with its attendant emphasis on healthy, capable children who will themselves become fully participating and valued members of the community.

The fight for special education under appropriate terms should thus be seen not simply as a dispute over how to handle needs the existence of which is taken for granted, but as part of a growing acknowledgment within the Hasidic community itself.[48] The community has increasingly been drawing a circle to keep these children in. The need for state support for special education, and its availability on terms other than those dictated solely by parents within the Hasidic community, made it vastly more complicated to act upon the growing acknowledgment of the value and special needs of handicapped children. Already stigmatized for their handicap, could they be forced to undergo the extra stigmatization that would surely attend their regular exposure to the secular community, an exposure shared by none of their fellow children? This extra dimension of internal stigmatization compounds the "trauma" and "mockery" at the hands of other public school children explicitly alluded to in the court papers (see Mintz 1992, 311).

Recognition of this dilemma is relevant to understanding the position of the dissenting group of Kiryas Joel residents. This faction's original and continuing motivation was loyalty to the ways of the deceased Reb Joel Teitlebaum. Their stance in the school board dispute took the form of active resistance to the education of Kiryas Joel's handicapped children under *any* state auspices, and was expressed in an *amicus* brief against the school board. Almost none of the parents of handicapped children in Kiryas Joel found it possible to continue sending their child to a "mixed" public school. The dissident group within Kiryas Joel further objected to separating the handicapped children within a public school whose curriculum had no religious character, even though that school consisted solely of children from Hasidic families. The separate school district arrangement still resulted in the handicapped children being educated according to fundamentally different cultural values than their nonhandicapped peers. It can thus plausibly be seen as a milder version of the exposure to double internal stigmatization we have just identified with regard to the sending of handicapped children to "mixed" public schools.[49]

Leonard Levy, commenting on the New York Court of Appeals ruling in *Grumet*, argues that the question of the children's best interests should have been paramount in the decision, yet it was not (1994). Concern for the children is expressed in Justice Stevens's concurrence, but not on terms we would expect from the considerations we have just outlined.

Stevens argues that the "panic, fear and trauma" of the students in the mixed public schools could have been alleviated by the state's taking steps to "teach . . . their schoolmates to be tolerant and respectful of Satmar customs."[50] Aside from the practical doubt whether such hypothetical "steps" would be effective, this recommendation once again ignores the double stigma placed on handicapped Hasidic children attending outside public schools. In any event, it appears that the main aspect of the children's welfare about which Stevens is concerned is that of "associating with their neighbors."[51] Stevens seems here to have lost sight of the fact that these are *handicapped* children: this assertion would be more appropriate in the context of a law journal debate about the constitutionality of any parochial schooling (Galanter 1966).[52]

Meanwhile the Satmar Hasidim of Kiryas Joel—a group of Jews closely knit in their daily relations, kin networks, and shared practices, but otherwise liable to sharp internal divisions—seek to preserve their group identity and simultaneously obtain government benefits in a manner that conforms to the religious sociology of Protestantism and to the religious establishment and equal protection concerns of constitutional jurisprudence. A new judicial resolution of the dispute should not come at the expense of their children's ability to receive special education in a setting consistent with the particular context of their lives.

Conclusion

Three major approaches are reflected in the Supreme Court opinions in *Kiryas Joel*. One is Scalia's rhetorical dismissal of the Establishment Clause complaint. A second, significant primarily because it reflects the heritage of Supreme Court jurisprudence in the post–World War II decades, is Stevens's almost nostalgic insistence on the handicapped children's overriding right to interact with non-Hasidic children from the surrounding area. The third is Souter's and O'Connor's narrowly technical reading of unconstitutionality, which appeared to permit the school board to continue once the New York legislature rewrote the enabling legislation in terms less specific to Kiryas Joel.

If there ever were a *Kiryas Joel II,* the Court would face a harder choice. Perhaps it might assert that, regardless of fine points of legislative procedure, the First Amendment commitment to free exercise of religious freedom may in certain situations entail a limitation of the power of the state to prevent local or parochial "establishments of religion." It might also admit that there are inevitable limitations on the free exercise of religion, when such free exercise is deemed incompatible with a predominant concern for preventing the establishment of religion. Based on the notions of polity and identity that have underlain constitutional jurisprudence until now, the Constitution may not be able to resolve the *Kiryas Joel* paradox. *Kiryas Joel* might well be an object lesson in the claim that "liberalism's deep structure precludes it from explaining and justifying the toleration of non-liberal cultures" (Lipkin 1995).

That so much debate centers on the case indicates not only that it is a hard one, but that it turns on central dilemmas of what we still call the American polity. *Kiryas Joel* presents a challenge to two underlying assumptions of constitutional jurisprudence: first, that political participation is determined according to territorial boundaries that are politically neutral in themselves; and second, that the subject of rights can always be specified as the individual person. It is impossible to predict whether or not constitutional jurisprudence will indeed prove flexible enough to accommodate a broader range of notions of identity than the schema of territoriality and individualism. It is clear, however, that such jurisprudence can and must be enriched by revelation of the particularity of the premises about personhood and belonging that have underlain constitutional interpretation until now. *Kiryas Joel* fosters such revelation by pressing the claims of an identity dependent on genealogical and diasporic loyalty rather than individual and territorial liberty.

Notes

Introduction

1. This dismissal of "the local" per se is misleading insofar as it suggests that the local is purely anecdotal, not susceptible to analysis in itself. Richard Ford has incisively articulated the power politics of local geography in an effort to dispel "two contradictory conceptions of local political space . . . One [of which] regards local jurisdictions as . . . administrative conveniences without autonomous political significance [while] [t]he other treats local jurisdictions as autonomous entities that deserve deference because they are manifestations of an unmediated democratic sovereignty" (1994, 1843–46). To further the possible comparison between the diasporic and the local suggested in our text, I would note that of these two conceptions, the latter—a kind of romanticization of a particular social form as "authentic" or "immediate"—could be extended to diasporas (the immigrant hometown society in the New World) as well as localities (the New England town meeting). The stress here on the *powers* of diaspora is meant in part to counter that very risk of romanticization.

2. One of these assumptions is that "international peace and security" (for example, in the context of the Program in International Peace and Security Studies sponsored by the MacArthur Foundation)

is a reasonable and achievable goal, as a refinement of the modern state-system.

3. Walzer's discussion of territoriality is aptly summarized by William Connolly: "This fusion of shared understandings with the territorial state as the fundamental unit of political membership constitutes the Walzerian space for democratic action. Beyond this boundary there are interstate and state/stateless relations, but not democratic politics. Since the overtly conceived hypothetical alternatives to this division are the anarchy of a universal market without states or the oppression of a world state, the reader (in a rich, powerful, democratic state) settles back into the comforting rhetoric of democratic politics inside a territorial state governed by shared understandings and common principles of membership" (1995, 148).

4. See Jon Stratton's *Coming Out Jewish* (2000) for provocative suggestions about how Jewish identity continues to trouble the liberal state project.

5. "Since no set of discrete territorial units—no matter how configured—can accommodate existing social, political, and economic arrangements, we need to consider the possibility of a multilayered and not strictly hierarchical appproach to governance in which the territorial notions that undergird decision making more closely reflect the different spatial structures in which issues and problems arise" (Murphy 1996, 84). Older visions along these lines have recently been evoked as well, such as those "'networks of mutual aid' dreamed about at the end of the nineteenth century by the anarchist geographer Peter Kropotkin" (Mattelart 1994, x). Meanwhile, Connolly insists that the state need not be the ideal limit of democracy: *"Some elements of a democratic ethos can extend beyond the walls of the state"* (1995, 155; emphasis in original). See also Anupam Chandar's proposal for a partial acknowledgment of the legal authority of homelands in certain diasporic contexts (Chandar 2001).

6. For an overview, see Cohen 1996; see also the contents of the journal *Diaspora*, edited by Khachig Tölölyan.

7. Skinner may have had in mind the unusually generous terms under which American Jews have been allowed to retain U.S. citizenship while sharing fully in the military duties of Israeli citizens as well.

8. The following paragraphs dealing with subcontinent Indians and Rom are not intended as an incomplete list in response to this question, but as examples that make clearer the question's ramifications.

9. "Communal," of course, has very different political valences among Indians and Jews.

10. This is a confusion indulged in by Weyrauch and Bell when they describe the island society of Tristan da Cunha, governed by a founding "partnership document . . . express[ing] a fundamental conception of absolute equality" (396), as an actualization of the world imagined by Robert Cover in his classic essay "Nomos and Narrative" (1983). Tristan da Cunha, as described by Weyrauch and Bell, is not only nonviolent, but also anomic and atextual, and recalls, if anything, the "original position" of a contractarian society described by John Rawls (1971). Cover, on the contrary, described communities that could maintain themselves without statist monopolies of legitimate violence precisely because they maintained a text-based nomos.

11. Similarly, groups making claims for autonomy are often forced to cast their history in spatial terms by the territorialist-nationalist framework of legitimating polities within which those claims are made (Hale 1994).

12. It is all too obvious that "indigenous" peoples have not generally fared well at the hands of "liberal" territorial states, yet a rich and painful summary of one such experience is germane here. "In 1887, Congress passed the General Allotment Act (ch. 119, 24 Stat. 388), a measure designed expressly to destroy what was left of the basic indigenous socioeconomic cohesion by eradicating traditional systems of collective land holding. Under provision of the statute, each Indian identified as such by demonstrating 'one-half or more degree of Indian blood' was to be issued an individual deed to a specific parcel of land—160 acres per family head, eighty acres per orphan or single person over eighteen years of age, and forty acres per dependent child—within existing reservation boundaries. Each Indian was required to accept U.S. citizenship in order to receive his or her allotment. Those who refused, such as a substantial segment of the Cherokee 'full-blood' population, were left landless. Generally speaking, those of mixed ancestry whose 'blood quantum' fell below the required level were summarily excluded from receiving allotments. In many cases, the requirement was construed by officials as meaning that an applicant's 'blood' had to have accrued from a single people. . . . In other instances, arbitrary geographic criteria were also employed; all Cherokees, Creeks and Choctaws living in

Arkansas, for example, were not only excluded from allotment, but permanently denied recognition as members of their separate nations" (Churchill 1996, 256).

This destruction of collective patterns of landholding is both analogous to, and an occasional aspect of, the forced individuation of genealogical communities by territorial states. In Palestine between the two world wars, Palestinian Arab lands were similarly subject to forced decollectivization, but there the purpose was to promote alienation of land and its sale to the Jewish Agency (Atran 1989). In both instances atomization of communal groups and their resources was part of the process of diasporization.

13. For an extraordinarily lucid analysis of what happens when such categorization is attempted, see Cohen 1996, 178.

14. McLean reinforces this trope, referring to "the diasporic discovery of Columbus" in his review of Todorov's book, *The Conquest of America* (McLean 1992–93, 9).

15. "[T]he conquest of America . . . heralds and establishes our present identity. . . . We are all the direct descendants of Columbus" (Todorov 1984, 5). Or an earlier voyager than Columbus: "Our history begins with the departure of Ulysses" (Nancy 1991, 10); see discussion in J. Boyarin 1994.

16. Thus Kalman Bland has criticized the way we use the word "diaspora," since we thereby use a "universal" Greek term for a range of experiences whose difference we want to leave space for. He suggests that we replace it by the Hebrew *galut,* since to him the latter implies not so much homelessness (and its correction through return), but the situation of displacement that is to be reflected on and not rejected. For us, however, *galut* has precisely the opposite affect, since it has very strong modernist-Zionist overtones; the Yiddish *goles* comes closer to what Bland is trying to say to us. If we could say *goles* rather than *galut,* we would then cite the common Yiddish saying *a yid iz in goles* as a desideratum for Jewishness, rather than merely a complaint about the unalterable fate of the Jews. That this is a plausible interpretation in the framework of Jewish hermeneutics is suggested by an analogous case in which Rabbi Moshe Feinstein, the greatest Jewish legal authority of the post–World War II decades, made a rabbinic decision partly on the basis of the verse "Its [the Torah's] paths are paths of peace." Rabbi Feinstein determined that a certain ruling would be inconsistent with the authority

of this verse, since that ruling would not be following "the path of peace."

17. "Diaspora theories are derived principally from the historically specific experience of 'the Black Atlantic,' a transnational unit of analysis that addresses the complex socioeconomic and cultural interconnections between the Caribbean, Europe, Africa and Afro-America" (Lavie and Swedenburg 1996, 14, citing the work of Paul Gilroy and Stuart Hall). This is an ambiguous statement. Certainly, as the references to Gilroy and to Hall show, what Gilroy calls the Black Atlantic has been a fruitful cultural topos in which to nurture a reinvigorated contemporary concept of diaspora. But the erasure of earlier diaspora histories *and* modes of reflection ("theories") here runs counter to a key thrust in Gilroy's (if not Hall's) work, namely, a generous attempt to begin articulating Black and Jewish modes of historical memory (Gilroy 1993, 187–223).

18. As does their idea of deterritorialization, developed in another book (Deleuze and Guattari 1986). We will say nothing of deterritorialization here, except that it once again implicitly assumes a *prior* condition of territoriality. See also Kronfeld 1996, 1–17.

19. An assertion questioned by the legal theorist and psychoanlyst Pierre Legendre (1985, 80).

20. Their chapter explicitly dealing with Jews is titled "587 B.C.–A.D. 70."

21. This adage of Benjamin Franklin's is grounded in an ultimately individualistic and voluntaristic notion of community, one at odds with the general experience of peoples in diaspora.

Tricksters, Martyrs, and Collaborators

1. This point has frequently been missed in non-Jewish readings of the stories of Ya'el and Judith, which take these as condemnations of the women.

2. For further discussion, see D. Boyarin 1997. It should be emphasized that references to femminization or self-femminization throughout are not intended to point to a "natural" femininity, but rather to the employment of the topoi of a particular cultural formation—hence, the neologism. See note 5.

3. Tobit is a fiction written in the Hellenistic period but dated back to the eighth century B.C.E. Levine acutely remarks that it is no accident that the protagonists of the narrative are of the tribe of

Naphtali, "which was geographically separated from the other Rachel tribes," and is accordingly always already diasporized "even in Palestine" (1992, 107): "Naphtali dwelt among the Canaanites, *the inhabitants of the land*" [Judges 5:18; emphasis mine, indeed]. See also Biale 1986, 14–15: "In terms of political rights, there was very little difference between the Jews of Palestine and those of the Diaspora, which originated in Babylonian times and spread throughout the Mediterranean under the Greeks and the Romans."

4. The other two involve imaginary geographies and an emphasis on genealogical purity: endogamy. Neither of these, of course, are irrelevant for the present project. If we do not treat them here, it is because we haven't worked out how to deal with them together. See, however, George Nickelsburg's apt remark (as paraphrased by Levine) that the focus on endogamy is "less a matter of ethnic purity than it is an argument against any 'arrogant disdaining of one's own people,' which then could lead to the loss of self-identity," upon which she comments, "However, when in-group and out-group are problematic categories, ethnic purity would not be an unexpected agendum" (Levine 1992, 108).

5. We use this artificial coinage, based on "femme" as in butch/femme, in order to indicate the constructed and nonessentialist character of the "feminization" imputed to these sociocultural practices. See also D. Boyarin 1997, 4, n.9.

6. The contrast between Douglas's and Bakhtin's respective responses to the grotesque would be, then, related to the particular historical-cultural formations that they focused on and not theoretically driven differences.

7. Cf. an analogous point in Modleski 1991, 95.

8. Words just don't mean what we want them to mean when we say them, as Gallop herself had written earlier (1982)!

9. "The structural linguistics that still underlies much poststructural analysis—signifier/signified—is simply allegory all over again. And it will always reproduce precisely this problem. Without the penis as signifier, we'd never know a phallus, so the dominant fiction *requires* taking penis for phallus. The same fiction, as allegorical metaphysics, *requires* we distinguish between them, or there would be nothing recognizable as *meaning* apart from signifiers" (Luxon 1995).

10. We also think that there is much of value in Cantor's book.

Although we don't accept it finally as plausible, we find interesting her notion that sex-dominating and -discriminating practices in traditional Judaism are a function of the "national emergency," and thus will naturally disappear with redemption. If redemption means nationalism, however, we are inclined to see exacerbation and not amelioration of male domination as its product.

11. As pointed out by Ben-Yehuda (passim), this element of the myth has nothing even in Josephus to back it up. In an earlier version of this argument, we uncritically accepted this version as if it were Josephus's and laid to Josephus's door values that he may very well have been attacking. According to Josephus, the siege was much shorter, and there were no battles at all before the end. This version, the one version purveyed in Israeli official culture and memory, is an entirely modern fabrication whose origin can be laid to a living man. It had us fooled, just as it initially did Ben-Yehuda himself.

12. Zerubavel's harrowing account of the use of Masada in early Zionist praxis and ideology (76–77) indicates how completely these are informed by European non-Jewish cultural norms. In contrast to the Zionist leader, Berl Katznelson, who considered the omission of Masada from Jewish historiography a sign of capitulation to external censorship (24), we would argue that there is a strong sense within which the modern mythicization of Masada constitutes such a capitulation to "foreign" cultural norms. Zerubavel remarks that "the silencing of Masada in rabbinical sources has in turn been silenced in Israeli collective memory" (203). Interestingly enough, although largely so, this is not an entirely accurate representation. There is one form in which the Masada story was preserved within Jewish memory, with perhaps fateful results. While it is traditional to observe that Josephus was hardly read among the Jews until modern times, there was a medieval literary connection, namely the Italian Hebrew pastiche of Josephus known as the Book of Josippon. In that book we find the story of Masada as the climax and finale to the narrative (Flusser 1981, 423–31). Carlin Barton and Daniel Boyarin (2000) argue that the version preserved in Josippon, in which the emphasis was on the sacrifice of the children as an antitype of the sacrifice of Isaac (actually sacrificed and resurrected in Ashkenazi tradition; see Spiegel 1967), was the determinative model leading to the child sacrifices by Jews (of their own children) during the Crusader maraudings.

13. Zerubavel points out early critical views of the account, especially that of Trude Weiss-Rosmarin (Zerubavel 1995, 198–200). Weiss-Rosmarin's explanation, that "Josephus fabricated this story in order to clear from his conscience his betrayal of his comrades during an earlier stage of the revolt," as well as Mary Smallwood's notion that "Josephus fabricated the suicide scene in order to cover up the Romans' barbaric behavior following the Masada people's surrender" are both compatible with the explanation that we will offer presently. Such a text is certainly overdetermined. For extensive discussion of the literature, see Zerubavel (198–203) and especially the notes appended thereto.

14. Erich Gruen suggested this comparison to me.

15. Israeli sociologist Nachman Ben-Yehuda describes his experience (in 1987!) of discovery that the Masada myth upon which he and all Israelis were brought up was a falsehood: "What was I supposed to do when it turned out that such a major element of my identity was based on falsehood, on a deviant belief?" (1995, 5). Ben-Yehuda is, moreover, studying the "Masada myth" as a deviation from Josephus's narrative, bracketing the issue of Josephus's own reliability, a procedure that makes sense for his goal. For the purposes of his method, termed "contextual constructionism," there has to be some objective point from which to deviate. He takes Josephus as such a point, which works for him whether or not Josephus's account is reliable, because it is, in fact, the only source for the entire event (29).

16. Ben-Yehuda's new book is devoted to answering just this question from a social scientific point of view.

17. For Masada the tourist trap, see Zerubavel 1995, 133–37.

18. This notion was, as Berkowitz has perspicaciously pointed out, a sort of topos of Zionist rhetoric: "The prevailing theme of thumbnail sketches was that he [Brandeis], like Herzl, Nordau, and a few other key leaders—reaching back to the Biblical Moses—had 'found his way back' to Judaism and the Jews; his life could easily be interpreted according to the Zionist theme of exile, return, and redemption" (1996, chapter 2). It can be seen clearly that Yadin is writing Josephus into this preexistent mythical pattern as well. No one seems to have seen the irony in the fact that nearly all of the activist leaders of Zionism were men [sic] who were culturally distant from Jewish tradition.

19. Unless, of course, Josephus's story is to be read as critical of the Masadans, in which case it is only Yadin and his fellows who have bought the "Roman" value system. Paul Breines points to a similar case: "Tough Jews also appear in the nooks and crannies. One finds them in a recent Giant Coloring Book for children, *The Story of Chanukah,* the final page of which offers a towering depiction of Judah Maccabee. Sword at the ready, this mighty defender of the Jews bears a notable resemblance to the evil warriors of the Syrian king Antiochus who appear in the book's opening pages—an easily overlooked moment in this children's book" (1990, 7).

20. For other voices that have mobilized this opposition, see Zerubavel 1995, 201–2; Ben-Yehuda 1995.

21. This is a wonderful joke. The century-later rabbinic rebel against the Romans, Bar Kokhba, was punningly dubbed Bar Kozba, Son of Lies! The text is cunningly creating a genealogy here. It is important to remember in this context that Bar Kokhba was also the nephew of a rabbi who counseled peace. For an entirely different interpretation of the joke, however, see Fränkel (1971, 84), according to whom the cognomen is given because of his willingness to help the rabbi deceive the Romans and not because of his earlier leadership of the thugs, implying that the text disapproves of the rabbi's ruse! This is a rare example, we think, within which Fränkel's political values have quite befogged his usually very sharp eyes. It should be mentioned that other manuscripts read "Father Dagger."

22. Supplied from eds.

23. Typically understood as referring to the Temple with reference to the verse: "the goodly mountain, the Lebanon" (Deut. 3:25), the goodly mountain being, of course, the Temple mount.

24. As Biale (1986, 23) has emphasized, this story is as much a myth as any other. According to Palestinian versions of the story, Rabbi Yoḥanan supported the revolt until it became apparent that it was hopeless. The issue is clearly not truth versus falsehood but the respective value systems of different myths. In addition, this point makes clear that we are not talking about a Jewish versus a non-Jewish value system but, as we have emphasized all along, putting the spotlight upon one system of values that diaspora Judaism developed in dialogue and dialectic with others. For discussion of other versions of this myth as they appear in rabbinic literature, see inter

alia Neusner 1970, and more critically Neusner 1981, 307–28, and Saldarini 1975.

25. Just to underline this point, in an earlier sequence of the same narrative text, the destruction of Jerusalem is ascribed to the unwillingness of another rabbi, a certain Rabbi Zecharia son of Avqulos, to kill a Jew who was informing on the rabbis to the Romans. As we will see, the rabbis make clear distinctions between accommodation that serves the purpose of continued life and Jewish existence and collaboration that destroys it.

26. As the case of Edelman makes clear, this surrender was hardly unique to Zionists; revolutionary Jewish socialists (to whom we feel much more allegiance) were also caught up in precisely the same imagery of "dignity" and "manliness." For excellent discussion, see Breines 1990, 131–32: "'At stake are our lives,' the Bundist, Chaim Helfand, concluded, 'and still more our honor and human dignity. We must not allow ourselves to be rounded up and slaughtered like oxen.'" Once more, we emphasize, it is not the first stake, life, that would put this utterance in conflict with the rabbis, but the second, the "still more." For the rabbis, it is the one who kills *without any hope of saving his or her own life* who has surrendered human dignity and become like an animal.

27. Much of the following discussion has appeared in other contexts with somewhat different emphases.

28. Interestingly enough, the verse explains that they are afraid of Israel, and *that* is the reason not to provoke them.

29. In a fascinating passage, Thomas Jefferson speculates on the fact that Native Americans have a different sense of honor from the "white man." In the passage, Jefferson is defending the male Native American from some European representations that effeminize him (represent him as having milk-bearing breasts!): "I am able to say, in contradiction to this representation, that he is neither more defective in ardor, nor more impotent with his female, than the white reduced to the same diet and exercise; that he is brave, when an enterprise depends on bravery; education with him making the point of honor consist in the destruction of an enemy by strategem, and in the preservation of his own person free from injury; or, perhaps, this is nature, while it is education which teaches us to honor force more than finesse" (quoted in Pearce 1988, 92–93).

30. In D. Boyarin 1999, 22–41, there is a much more detailed reading of this passage in its larger historical context.

31. Literally, "the stairs leading up to the place of judgment"; this is one of the structures that the Mishna forbids Jews to participate in the building of.

32. That is, the provincial governor serving as judge.

33. The references to Jesus, found in both manuscripts, are deleted in the printed editions, as have nearly all such references since the first editions, owing to the Italian censors.

34. As Len Kaplan has reminded us, rabbinic theodicy is remarkably like that of Job's (discredited) friends. This latter is, however, not unlike the deuteronomistic theodicies. Daniel had previously, in fact, made this very point. The verses in which Job's friends insist that God does not punish without cause are quoted positively in midrash, e.g., at Mekilta, Masekta d'Amaleq 1, where this position is presented as if it were the view of the implied author of Job. This aspect of rabbinic religiosity leads some modern orthodox rabbis to insist that the Nazi genocide must have been punishment for the collective sins of the Jewish people (usually *either* support of *or* opposition to Zionism). Secular Jews have frequently, it seems, misunderstood this as an attempt to demonize opponents rather than the desperate endeavor to maintain God's justice.

35. This insistence on God's justice carries with it, of course, the constant danger of a self-righteous judgment of others who are suffering. While this danger is often enough realized in actual religious life, we hardly think that it was the intent or mood of the Talmud.

36. For the topos of the warp as female and the woof as male and weaving as sexual intercourse, see Scheid and Svenbro 1996, 87.

37. It is at least worth noting that in this Jewish representation, manumission was considered a sign of adherence to Torah and disloyalty to Roman authority. It is not at all clear to me what the historical background for this judgment could be. However, issues surrounding Galatians 2:28, 1 Corinthians 7, and Philemon seem relevant in this matter. If Jewish and Christian resistance to the Roman order consisted of overturning the hierarchies that subtended the society, then freeing slaves might indeed have been a subversive act. See also Perkins 1995, 139.

38. In Talmudic style, negative predicates are nearly always put into third person sentences in order to avoid, in a situation in which

the text was read out loud, predicating them of the speaker or his interlocutors, so "that man" frequently has to be translated as "I" or as "you."

39. The gendered meaning of these tactics may be inferred from the context of Polemo's writing as described by Gleason. Much later we find anti-Semites writing that "Jews were incapable of martyrdom. In the face of death they screamed, cursed, and defended themselves. . . . In 1895, the Italian journalist Paolo Orano contrasted the supposed Jewish fear of death, avarice, pacifism, and lack of spirituality to the Christian and Roman spirit" (Mosse 1985, 150).

40. For the "manliness" of the martyr, see the martyrdom of Polycarp, as cited in Wiedemann 1992, 80.

41. It is not clear what biblical reference is intended. We wonder if perhaps it is not Pinḥas the son of Elʿazar (Numbers 25:11) whom they have in mind here. His activities were certainly phallic and "manly," i.e., murderous. He killed by driving a stake into the bodies of a sinning couple. Elʿazar himself is portrayed as having military functions, e.g., at Numbers 31:21. Another, perhaps more likely possibility, is that the 4 Maccabees text, produced quite late in antiquity, refers paradoxically to its own story, such that Elʿazar had already become such a compelling symbol of brave martyrdom that the later telling of the story can refer to the earlier as a virtual intertext, with Elʿazar serving as the true type of himself. This interpretation is further supported by the text of 2 Maccabees, which already knows that Elʿazar is to become an example and reminder of virtue for generations to come.

42. As Davis observes, Rabbi Ḥanina's virtue, as that of his wife and daughter as articulated above, was precisely about accepting God's judgment, and here, paradoxically, it is his interlocutor who claims that he has not sufficiently submitted himself to that very judgment (Davis 1994).

43. See also Lieberman 1939–1944, 416.

44. There are elements in this story, for instance the chastity test, that are strikingly like topoi of the Hellenistic romances, for instance Achilles Tatius's *Leucippe and Clitophon.* Indeed, in another of the Hellenistic romances, Xenophon's *Ephesian Tale,* the heroine is sent to a brothel and avoids her brothel duties through feigning sickness (Perkins 1995, 57–58), and in Tatius, the heroine avoids violation through the excuse that she is menstruating, a claim that Goldhill

claims is unique in Greek literature (116). The generic connections of the Talmudic Haggadah need much further research.

45. Indeed, I believe that this formulation is more consonant with Davis's argument itself. Incidentally, this topos of the "virgin in the brothel" provides an elegant example of the different meanings that a cultural item has within different discursive contexts. For Christian usages of this topos, see Gravdal 1991, 22–23. Rashi's version of the fate of Beruriah is a version of the "seduction" plot discussed by Gravdal on the same page.

46. For an example of the persistence (deflated, of course) of this "doubled consciousness," see the sensitive commentary on *Portnoy's Complaint* in Gottfried 1988, 40–41. Gottfried remarks that "to be truly American in these terms is to reject one's ethnicity and its more fluid gender possibilities in favor of assimilation and its more rigid conception of American maleness" (41). We will argue that the rabbinic situation in the Roman and Parthian Empire was powerfully analogous to that in which an American Jewish boy would learn one set of gender norms at home and another "from the radio."

47. Grant Allen, quoted in Reynolds and Humble 1993, 41. Note that there is actually tension within this text between indications that the situation of male dominance is natural and that it is historical: "It must always be so," followed immediately by "for many years to come"; but finally we come to something that is "deep down in the very roots of the idea of sex."

48. Quoted in Craft 1995, 73. On Ruskin see Dellamora 1990, 117–29.

49. Wiedemann (1992, 65–66) makes clear the appropriateness of analogies between Roman and Victorian cultural conditions. Of course, this is partly the case because the Victorian imperialists modeled themselves and their self-representation on notions of the "Roman."

50. In part it reflects a controversy between Martin Buber and Franz Rosenzweig, and my position is close to the "metaphysical anti-Zionism" of the latter, while Buber, "as the intellectual leader of the struggle for Jewish adult education in Israel, has waged a difficult struggle his whole life to ensure normal circumstances for the community of the people, so that it may prove its chosenness within and not outside those circumstances. To him and to religious Zionists in *this* sense, chosenness seems, so to speak, too easy if it is bound up

with the circumstances of Diaspora existence. There it can very comfortably become an ideology, a real 'ideological superstructure' in the Marxist sense; it preaches the virtues of quality and liberty, of tolerance and humanity, of love for one's neighbour, near and distant, because in this way the benefit of the Jewish minority is preserved. The fulfillment of these virtues by the majority makes the existence of the minority possible. Not until the Jews had their own political responsibility can or could it be seen how much true sincerity there was in these Jewish demands for tolerance. A Zionism understood in this sense does not therefore decide only on its own moral appearance and the internal Jewish constitution of the community it has established, it also judges retrospectively to what degree those demands of the generation of the Diaspora were genuine" (Simon 1956, 103). Our argument against Buber is precisely focused at the point at which political dominance is read as "normal," while being dominated (or at any rate, not dominating) is then "abnormal," whereas we are claiming that political domination, like economic domination, produces mystifying "ideology"—the phallus—to maintain itself, while being nondominant is a place from which knowledge of different meanings for the masculine body is generated. Furthermore, one might put the following question to Buber: what is it that constitutes "the Jews" if not a given political and economic situation? In other words, could we not say that precisely what constructs "the Jew" is the diaspora condition that ex hypothesi produces certain ethical virtues? Otherwise it seems Buber is falling precisely into a "völkisch" way of thinking that he is precisely at pains to avoid (cf. Goldstein 1957, 248).

51. Seen in this light, the origins of (Western) Zionism with its (in)famous ideology of "Muscle Jews" lie not so much in the "anomalies" of the Jewish condition as in the same late Victorian process that produced "Muscular Christianity" (Hall 1994) as well.

52. This point is made by Virginia Burrus about early Christianity: "For men, the pursuit of Christian ascesis entailed the rejection of public life and therefore of the hierarchies of office and gender; in this respect, their opponents were not far off the mark when they insinuated that male ascetics were 'feminized' through their rejection of the most basic cultural expressions of male identity" (1995, "Agnes").

53. Lori Lefkowitz has put it well: "In Hebrew Scriptures, it is

not the older, stronger, more masculine son who inherits the future. Instead, in the cases of Isaac and Ishmael, Jacob and Esau, Joseph and his brothers, later King David and his brothers, and Solomon and his brothers, it is the younger son, often the child of the more beloved but less fertile wife, the physically smaller, less hirsute, more delicate, more domestic son, the son closer to the mother, a hero of intellect rather than of brawn who will be chosen by God over his brothers. In most cases this son is the mother's rather than the father's favorite. The Law of the Mother. An awareness of this pattern may have contributed to an image of the Jews as a feminized people ruled by their women" (1988, 20–21).

54. Similarities to wise Jewish courtier tales from the Book of Esther onward are not accidental.

55. In fact, these same services are those performed by slaves for their masters as well. This point only serves to reinforce the ways that the wife's relation to her husband is inscribed in this culture as benevolent and valorized (voluntary/involuntary) servitude.

56. On the other hand, an opposing argument could be made as well, namely, that freely adopted servility (if it is not a mere sham) by socially powerful people is subversive of power orders, while, of course, the forced servility of socially weak people is an effect of their oppression.

57. However, for slaves it seems, it was precisely dependence on other males that was honored. Slaves have something to teach us about demystifying masculinist ideologies. Dale Martin has derived some fascinating evidence to this effect from inscriptions: "The very names of slaves and freedpersons and the epithets they accepted for themselves demonstrate their acceptance of patronal ideology: many slaves were named Philodespotos, 'master-lover,' and one freedman is complimented as being a master-loving man in spite of the fact that this very term occurs in literary sources as an insult similar to 'slavish.' Several slaves honored a deceased fellow slave by saying he was a real lord-lover *(philokyrios)*. They bear, *probably without shame,* names that bespeak servitude, for example, Hope-bearer, Pilot, Gain, Well-wed, and Changeable" (1990). For a counter-example, see ibid., 43. Before rushing to dub such data as mere evidence of false consciousness, we would do well to examine our own ideological investments, investments that still, as in Greek times, validate "tops" over "bottoms" (Bersani 1995, 14). We are assuming

that these namings and honorings belong to a relatively safe space of private discourse (discourse offstage) on the part of the slaves. Otherwise, they might be only the sort of public-feigned performance from the analysis of which, Scott remarks, we are "likely to conclude [falsely] that subordinate groups endorse the terms of their subordination and are willing, even enthusiatic, partners in that subordination" (1990, 4).

58. Tal Ilan has demonstrated that in early Palestinian literature, Matrona is a proper name of a probably actual Jewish woman engaged in the study of Genesis, which was later understood, especially in the Babylonian texts, as the generic name for a Roman lady (1995, *Jewish Women*, 200–204; 1995, "Matrona").

59. This interpretation occurs so frequently that it can be regarded as almost a topos.

60. This is not an essential, automatic meaning for circumcision. Indeed, in some cultures, circumcision may have the opposite sense of removing that which is "female," the invaginating foreskin, from the body, thus rendering it wholly "male." We do not know what meanings circumcision had in biblical culture, but are arguing from hints within the cultural context of late antique rabbinic culture that *there* it was understood as a feminizing, not masculinizing, modification of the body, thus conforming to the famous Bettelheimian paradigm (Bettelheim 1954). For excellent discussion, see Caldwell 1987.

61. Eilberg-Schwartz 1994 is a detailed and thorough account of these issues and texts and should be consulted. Eilberg-Schwartz seems, however, to tend to regard these femminizations as problematic for men, while, in the spirit of Paul Gilroy, we see them as portending, however inchoately, the possibilities for a transcendence of masculinity. Gilroy writes, "It seems important to reckon with the limitations of a perspective which seeks to restore masculinity rather than work carefully towards something like its transcendence" (1993, 194). One's evaluation of circumcision will depend in part, I think, on whether one is seeking a restoration of masculinity or its transcendence, which does not, I add, imply transcendence of the body but indeed its very opposite.

62. In recent work, Nicole Loraux (and before her Froma Zeitlin) on the Greek side, and Carlin Barton on the Roman side, have been demonstrating how inadequate simple-minded binary oppositions of male and female are in describing Greco-Roman cultures as a whole

(Loraux 1995; Zeitlin 1996; Barton 1994). On the other hand, subjected populations such as the Jews would have met their others precisely in the political realm within which, as Loraux holds, these oppositions held more firmly.

63. It could be easily argued, however, that in contemporary Israel in certain religious quarters such generalized racism directed against gentiles, now Arabs, has been extended.

64. We specify "late antique" to emphasize, once more, that it is not an unhistoricized Jewish essence that we are claiming but a particular cultural moment, one that appeared in the Talmud, was muted but not extinguished in the Middle Ages, and reappeared in full force in Eastern Europe in the eighteenth and nineteenth centuries, as argued in D. Boyarin 1997.

65. This imagery was, of course, totally reversed in modern Zionist imagination. In a fascinating account, Yael Zerubavel has shown how a "myth" about Bar Kochba defeating, and then befriending, a lion was invented in the 1920s by Zionist educators and gradually became accepted as if it were an ancient legend and as an explicit figure of contrast to the Jews of Europe who were "led like sheep to the slaughter" (1995, 105-7).

66. It is important to note that, according to Jewish law, thieves are never executed but only required to make restitution with a fine.

67. The connection of this impermeable body with political power has recently been underscored once again by Carole Pateman: "The body of the 'individual' is very different from women's bodies. His body is tightly enclosed within boundaries, but women's bodies are permeable, their contours change shape and they are subject to cyclical processes. All these differences are summed up in the natural bodily process of birth. Physical birth symbolizes everything that makes women incapable of entering the original contract and transforming themselves into the civil individuals who uphold its terms. Women lack neither strength nor ability in a general sense, but, according to the classic contract theorists, they are naturally deficient in a specifically *political* capacity, the capacity to create and maintain political right" (1988, 96).

68. This pattern repeats itself in Babylonian rabbinic literature. It is not, therefore, a deviation from type.

69. We are mobilizing Mary Douglas's formative insight here as to the homology between practices relating to the individual body

and cultural and social problems relating to the body of the group (1980). Whereas she, however, was primarily concerned with such practices that defend the body, and thus the body-politic, from impurity, we are finding here a set of symbolic representations that at least partially overcome the confines between the Jewish body and the world.

70. In other words, if you are called to serve as an official of the Roman government, leave town!

Circumscribing Constitutional Identities in Kiryas Joel

1. All citations in the text to the Supreme Court's decision will be from the version published in 114 S. Ct. 2481 (1994).

2. In Yiddish, *Rov* in this context refers to the rabbi of a town, *Rebbe* to the leader of a group of Hasidim. Rabbi Teitlebaum had been the rabbi of the town of Satu Maru in Hungary, but as the leader of Hasidim, he was also thought of and hence eventually referred to as "Rebbe."

3. *School Dist. of Grand Rapids v. Ball,* 473 U.S. 373 (holding that supplementary classes provided at public expense to religious school students at the religious schools violated the Establishment Clause).

4. *Aguilar v. Felton,* 473 U.S. 402, 105 S. Ct. 3232 (holding that New York City's use of federal funds to pay public school employees to teach educationally deprived children in parochial schools violated the Establishment Clause because of inevitable excessive entanglement of church and state). This decision was reversed by the Supreme Court a decade later in *Agustini v. Felton,* 521 U.S. 203, 117 S. Ct. 1997 (holding that such a program did not violate the Establishment Clause). Justice O'Connor wrote in her 1997 opinion that "Our most recent cases have undermined the assumptions upon which *Ball* and *Aguilar* relied."

5. "Chapter 241 of the Laws of 1994 amends Section 1504 of the Education Law, to permit every city, town or village, in existence as of the effective date of the amendment, wholly within a single central or union free school district, but whose boundaries are not coterminous with the boundaries of such school district, to organize a new union free school district consisting of the entire territory of such municipality whenever the educational interests of the community require it if certain additional requirements are fulfilled (See

Education Law, Section 1504 [3])" (*Grumet v. Cuomo*, 625 N.Y.S. 2d 1000, 1003 [S. Ct. Albany Cty] [1995]).

6. 225 A.D.2d 4, 647 N.Y.S. 2d 565 (3d Dep't 1996), at 9. The Appellate Division found that the criteria in the new law were in fact designed to apply only to the Kiryas Joel situation and "further[ed] no known educational purpose" (id. at 6). It did not take issue with Justice O'Connor's prescription, but stated that her formula would only have been met "[h]ad the current law permitted any existing municipality, or even any village, to form a school district if it obtained appropriate approvals and also fulfilled statutory criteria designed to evidence a special educational need for a separate school district" (id. at 12).

7. See Witte 1996 (citations from the end of the eighteenth century identifying range of toleration with the varieties of Christian beliefs). The frequent emphasis on religious voluntarism in constitutional jurisprudence is identified by Witte primarily with the evangelical view and Enlightenment thought, two of the four major strands (along with Puritanism and civic republicanism) that contributed toward policies on religious freedom in the early United States (id. at 382, 383). "Those lofty protections of individual religious rights went hand-in-hand with the close restrictions on corporate religious rights that were also advocated by enlightenment exponents" (id. at 385).

8. "With a general Protestant ethos underlying society, government could remain separate from any particular church without unnaturally constricting the contribution made to public life by the citizenry's general religious values" (Berg 1995, 442). Subsequently, however, "[t]he vigorous pursuit of these aspects of separation in the context of an active state created the fundamental problem of Religion Clause interpretation: it put nonestablishment at war with free exercise" (id. at 443).

Few Protestant groups have relied solely on recruitment of individual adults to sustain themselves, and thus the association of Protestantism with pure individualism can easily be overstated. In terms of constitutional jurisprudence, however, the exception goes some distance toward proving the rule here. Thus the Supreme Court ruled in *Wisconsin v. Yoder* that Amish families could not be forced to send their children to school beyond the eighth grade. Yet in his dissent, Justice Douglas insisted that "Where the child is mature enough to express potentially conflicting desires, it would be an invasion of the child's rights to permit such an imposition without canvassing his views. . . . And, if an Amish child desires to attend high school, and is mature enough to have that desire respected, the State may well be able to override the parents' religiously motivated objections" (*Wisconsin v. Yoder,* 406 U.S. 205, 242, 92 S. Ct. 1526, 1547 [J. Douglas, dissenting in part]). I see Douglas's *Yoder* dissent as one of the sources of Justice Stevens's concurrence in *Kiryas Joel.*

9. Berg 1995, 448, citing Pildes and Niemi 1993.

10. Tribal "governments" are not based on principles of individualism and neutral territory. See, e.g., Clastres 1987. Such face-to-face groups do not confront complex questions of representation. One alternative model, which cannot be explored in detail here, is the Ottoman Empire's strategy of representation by ethnic communities within the territory of the empire: "What characterizes the [Ottoman Empire] is the extraordinarily active and vastly heterogeneous diasporic activity that is constantly afoot on its terrain" (Spivak 1990). For an extended reconsideration of the principle of "one nation per state" in the context of *Kiryas Joel* and *Shaw v. Reno,* see Blacksher 1995–96, 444–49.

11. Two of the key elements of the democratic, territorial state, according to Connolly, are "the recognition of a people (or nation) on [a contiguous] territory, bound together by a set of shared understandings, identities, debates, and traditions that, it is said, makes possible a common moral life and provides the basis upon which citizen/alien and member/stranger are differentiated; [and] the organization of institutions of electoral accountability and constitutional restraint that enable the territorialized people with shared understandings to rule themselves while protecting fundamental interests and freedoms" (1995, 136).

12. The papers and commentaries refer to the residents variously as "the Satmar," "the Satmar Hasidim" (most commonly), and "the Satmarer Hasidim" (which is closest to the Yiddish designation for the group).

13. Wheeler 1995, 242, citing *Kiryas Joel,* 114 S. Ct. at 2492 note 9, which quotes Brief for Petitioner Board of Education of Kiryas Joel at 4 n. 1 (emphasis added).

14. No advance is made by simply contrasting individual rights to group rights, since this sets up a dichotomy between the "indi-

vidual" and the "group." See, e.g., Brownstein 1990, 149: "Religions represent communities as well as individual identities." Because the boundaries of the individual and of the group are at stake within and beyond Kiryas Joel, Brownstein's remark brings us no closer to an understanding of the links among "religion," identity, and polity.

15. *Kiryas Joel* at 2489.

16. In a key passage Cover takes the contemporary Mennonites as exemplary of such nonstate nomic orders: "the Mennonite community creates law as fully as does the judge. First, the Mennonites inhabit an ongoing *nomos* that must be marked off by a normative boundary from the realm of civil coercion, just as the wielders of state power must establish their boundary with a religious community's resistance and autonomy. Each group must accommodate in its own normative world the objective reality of the other. There may or may not be synchronization or convergence in their respective understandings about the normative boundary and what it implies. But from a position that starts as neutral—that is, nonstatist—in its understanding of law, the interpretations offered by judges are not necessarily superior" (1983, 28).

17. *Bob Jones University v. United States,* 461 U.S. 574, 103 S. Ct. 2017 (1983).

18. "Kiryas Joel presents perhaps the most appealing constitutional case for a special school district (or other grant of local political power) for a distinct group: the group is a minority, it is religious (and thereby nomic), and it has exited a heterogenerous setting precisely to establish a separate nomos" (Greene 1996, 43). See also Minow 1995, "Constitution." Christopher Eisgruber uses the term "ethical diversity" rather than "nomos," but apologizes (perhaps tongue in cheek) for the substitution (1996, 88).

19. Suzanne Stone argues that Cover's alternative model of the Jewish relation to identity in and through law is of only limited potential application to a liberal jurisprudence such as that of the United States. "According to Jewish legal tradition, many Jewish legal principles are neither appropriate nor necessary for conventional politics because these principles are tied to particularist religious ideals" (1993, 813, 821 n. 39).

20. "They believe in a literal interpretation of the Torah" (Wheeler 1995, 224). Literal interpretation of the Torah is disavowed by rabbinic Judaism, which dictates instead rigorous reliance on a long

tradition of authoritative *interpretation*. Nor, for that matter, do Christian fundamentalists necessarily believe in a literalist reading of the Bible (see Stolzenberg 1993, 615). Yet that misconception seems the most likely source of Wheeler's distortion of the actual, and more nearly accurate, statement in *Kiryas Joel*: "They interpret the Torah strictly" (*Kiryas Joel* at 2485).

21. "*Sherbert* and its progeny defined the pressure to act *in violation of a religious command* as the paradigmatic free exercise burden" (Stolzenberg 1993, 601).

22. Thus, for example, Brownstein discusses the relation between establishment and free exercise in linear terms, claiming to "attack the problem of finding a middle ground at its roots by developing a doctrinal foundation for determining when the accommodation of free exercise rights ends and the prohibition of establishment clause preferences begins" (1990, 90); *also,* "the free exercise principle defines the limits of the anti-establishment principle" (Neuchterlein 1990, 1146). It is equally plausible to speak in terms of "a delicate and elusive balance" (Seal 1995, 1668), rather than tension, but here balance and tension effectively function the same way. Both strategies envision the ideal possibility of specifying that narrow appropriate space wherein the distinction between the realms of the two clauses can be discerned.

Another dilemma in First Amendment religious rights jurisprudence can be traced to the individualist bias. It seems natural enough to identify the establishment of religion with collectives, and free exercise with individual rights. "Rights of free exercise are quintessentially rights of autonomy. . . . [They are about] living in accord with one's deepest presuppositions about humankind and nature" (Lupu 1987, 422). Since *Kiryas Joel* is neither about "one's . . . presuppositions" nor about personal autonomy, but about a generational community, it seems inevitably to be about the Establishment Clause, not the Free Exercise Clause. Indeed, it has been suggested that the decision in *Kiryas Joel* was right as an Establishment Clause case, but that the case should have been brought as a free exercise case (Schweitzer 1995, 1029–30). If this is so, it is another example of the jurisprudential constraints to which the representatives of the village fit their case, to their own disadvantage.

Alternatively, free exercise may be associated with "exit" (not in the sense of a literal move away from society, but in the preservation of religious distinction through social detachment, as in *Yoder*), while the attempt by a religious group to retain certain perquisites of "proximity" by obtaining social benefits available from the government will be considered in the framework of establishment, as in *Kiryas Joel* (see Kuhns 1995, 1665–66). This will hardly be a principle adequate to the range of claims adjudicated under the constitutional rubric of "religion." By declaring what is done away from the broader society (even by a collective) as "private" free exercise, and what is done in interaction with the broader society as "establishment," it essentially extends outward the Protestant notion of the freedom of individual, private conscience.

23. "Because the line between lifting a burden and conferring a benefit depends so crucially upon perspective, the line serves as an unreliable and inappropriate measure of the constitutionality of government action" (Jacobs 1995, 169).

24. *Kiryas Joel* at 2484.

25. Kuhns 1995, 1599; Schweitzer 1995, 1007; Seal 1995, 1642; Wheeler 1995, 223. "The Satmar are the most ascetic sect of the Hasidim" (Thomas 1994, 532–33); "the Satmarer Hasidim, a sect of the Jewish faith . . . The Satmarer, in addition to separation from an outside community, practice separation between sects *[sic]* and follow a male and female dress code. Radio, vision *[sic]*, and publications in English are not widely used." The substitution of "sects" for "sexes" and of "vision" for "television" are obviously copyediting errors, not ethnographic inaccuracies. Nevertheless, the fact that they slipped through the careful editorial scrutiny of the author and his fellow law students suggests that a canned and stereotyped description of the Satmar Hasidim has been formulated. Similarly noteworthy is Acklin's reference to the village itself as a (presumably collective) religious actor: "The Village of Kiryas Joel (Village), a religious enclave of Satmar Hasidim, practices a strict form of Judaism" (Acklin 1995, 43). Budding legal scholars' reliance on outmoded ethnographies may be the cause of other distortions, such as the claim that "the Satmar Hasidic sect . . . eschew all modern conveniences such as . . . cars" and the exoticizing suggestion that they are "considered strangers in the Jewish community" (Hempen 1995, 1403), both quotes evidently interpolating information gleaned from Rubin 1972.

26. Even Souter's initial reference to the Satmar as practitioners

of strict Judaism may be misleading, insofar as it may be taken to mean that Satmar is a subset of the "Jewish faith." Describing the Satmar nomos as a form of Judaism might imply a particular heightened standing for other groups designating themselves as Jewish when appearing as *amici* in a case involving Satmar Hasidim. As suggested before, much of the liberal Jewish organizations' motivation can be explained by their continuing belief that a truly individual-regarding liberal state is the best guarantor of the safety of people such as Jews. That belief is not necessarily shared by diasporist-integrist Jewish communities like Satmar. Such communities are less likely to share general liberal assumptions about a tendency toward increasing rationalization of society and increasing recognition of human and civil rights, and partly for that reason are less likely to make Kantian or Rawlsian investments in a vision of the general good. Given that the dispute concerned the putative establishment of religion by the small and local group of Satmar Hasidim in Kiryas Joel, it is worth recalling that while even the name of Satmar reflects particularity rather than any universal pretensions, the names of the liberal organizations imply generality and hence a greater tendency toward the articulation of nationwide norms regarding religion.

The joint *amicus* brief in support of respondents was filed in the name of the American Jewish Congress, the National Jewish Community Relations Advisory Council, People for the American Way, the General Conference of Seventh-Day Adventists, and the Union of American Hebrew Congregations.

27. See the lists of terms associated by *Roget's Thesaurus* with "sectarian [n] *person who is narrow-minded*": adherent, bigot, cohort, disciple, dissenter, dissident, dogmatist, extremist, fanatic, henchman/woman, heretic, maverick, misbeliever, nonconformist, partisan, radical, rebel, revolutionary, satellite, schismatic, separatist, supporter, true believer, zealot; and with "sectarian [adj] *narrow-minded, exclusive*": bigoted, clannish, cliquish, dissident, doctrinaire, dogmatic, factional, fanatical, hidebound, insular, limited, local, nonconforming, nonconformist, parochial, partisan, provincial, rigid, schismatic, skeptical, small-town, splinter.

28. "The Grand Rebbe [Joel Teitelbaum] would be astounded to learn that after escaping brutal persecution and coming to America with the modest hope of religious tolerance for their ascetic form of Judaism, the Satmar had become so powerful, so closely allied with

Mammon, as to have become an 'Establishment' of the Empire State" (*Kiryas Joel* at 2506 [Scalia, J., dissenting]).

29. Lupu links Cuomo's support for the creation of the village school district and Cuomo's support for "a taxpayer-financed 'bereavement fund' for the Crown Heights Hasidic community after the death of its revered Rebbe, Menachem Schneerson" (1996, 118). Only from outside is it plausible to characterize the Lubavitch community in Crown Heights and the Satmarers of Williamsburg or Kiryas Joel as part of a single Hasidic community. Minow is aware of the rift between Satmar and Lubavitch; see her quaint suggestion that "given the historical tensions between the Satmar and Lubavitch Hasidic communities, an intriguing experiment in integration would bring Lubavitch children with disabilities into the Kiryas Joel public school" (1995, "Constitution," 23). There is something repugnantly unrealistic about this suggestion. One may share the values of integration and inclusion, yet question here (as we also do regarding Justice Stevens's dissent) why children with disabilities should be the subject of such experiments merely because they are entitled to and need state services.

30. Lupu 1996, 112 n. 7, see also 116. Lupu acknowledges that such extra-record considerations should not have influenced the Supreme Court's decision.

31. Unlike Justice Scalia's summary dismissal of the notion that a group like the Satmar Hasidim could "establish" religion in America, Justice Bellacosa of the New York Court of Appeals noted carefully in his dissent there that "no claim is made of any alleged restrictive covenants among the village's property owners, or of any alleged irregularity in the conduct of municipal or school district elections" (*Grumet* at 113 [J. Bellacosa dissenting]). One might say Justice Bellacosa was being obtuse or formalistic. We are suggesting that how to deal with such claims may depend substantially, and legitimately, on how and where they are raised. "The proper action would have been to sue to enjoin the coercive actions, not to strike down an independent piece of legislation that is secular on its face and in its operation" (Berg 1995, 499). After all, while the commitment of nomic communities to American constitutionalism may be questioned, it is a settled principle of Jewish diasporic communities that *dina de-malkhuta dina*—the law of the state is [binding] law.

32. *Kiryas Joel* at 249.

33. Aloofness has been part of the public depiction of the Satmar Hasidim in America at least since the publication of Rubin 1972.

34. Judge Bellacosa of the New York Court of Appeals, dissenting from that court's ruling on the unconstitutionality of the district, argued that if the village was constitutional, so was the district (*Grumet* at 113).

35. Ford makes the same point that Judge Bellacosa did in *Grumet*—that municipal and school district boundaries should be held to the same standard—but to opposite effect (1994, 1857ff.).

36. *Kiryas Joel* at 2496 (O'Connor, J., concurring). An instructive comparison is the establishment of the Village of Airmont in recent years out of a portion of the Town of Ramapo in Rockland County, New York, by an association of homeowners (including a number of non-Orthodox Jewish members) concerned about Ramapo's adoption of zoning measures favorable to Hasidic Jews, including "multiple-family housing in areas zoned for single family residences . . . [and] the allowance of home synagogues ('shteebles') in residential areas" (*Le Blanc-Sternberg v. Fletcher,* 972 F. Supp. 959, 960 [1995]).

37. *Kiryas Joel* at 2511 (J. Scalia, dissenting).

38. "Under New York law, a territory with at least 500 residents and not more than five square miles may be incorporated upon petition by at least 20 percent of the voting residents of that territory or by the owners of more than 50 percent of the territory's real property. N.Y. Village Law §§ 2-200, 2-202 (McKinney 1973 and Supp. 1994)" (*Kiryas Joel* at 2504 [Kennedy, J., concurring]).

39. Ford cites *Wright v. Council of Emporia,* 407 U.S. 451 (1972), holding that "local officials could not be enjoined from carving a new school district from an existing district that had not been desegregated" (1994, 1905–6).

40. See *Shelley v. Kraemer,* 334 U.S. 1, 22 (1948).

41. *Kiryas Joel* at 2504. The reference to electoral lines entails an analogy to the previous term's decision in *Shaw v. Reno,* as pointed out by Berg 1995, 489. Berg argues the importance of Kennedy's failure "to point out . . . that the special school district fell within the guidelines of *Shaw.* The New York legislature drew a district that was compact and contiguous, reflecting the lines of an existing political subdivision, the village. If Shaw is taken seriously, those facts

should be crucial. Shaw rests on and redoubles the commitment that the primary guideline for districting in America should be geography, that is, the location where people choose to live" (492). The last sentence here relies on the assumption that people's geographical situation, as a matter of choice, is the principle determinant of their political identity. In support of the localist principle, Abner Greene draws on Michael Walzer's argument that since "politics is always territorially based . . . [t]he democratic school should be an enclosure within a neighborhood: a special environment within a known world, where children are brought together as students exactly as they will one day come together as citizens" (1996, 50, quoting Walzer 1983, 225). Greene's reliance on "exit" allows him to have his cake and eat it too; for Greene, once a group of people have sufficiently demonstrated their commitment to their separate group existence by physical removal, they should be allowed social separatism as well. What troubles one respondent to Greene in particular, and more generally motivates those troubled by the implications of the Kiryas Joel district, is precisely the fear that those schooled parochially will, when they become adults, only "come together as citizens" for the furtherance of parochial interests.

42. Would the establishment of a separate village withstand a constitutional test if it appeared patently designed to establish an "all-white" municipality in part of a preexisting municipality already divided into black and white neighborhoods? That is, how far does the right of "almost any group" to create their own village extend? Applying Kennedy's analogy from the requirement for state action in equal protection cases to cases involving religious establishment might suggest that under New York's law, the voluntary separation of a group of white citizens would be upheld, regardless of racist intent.

43. 413 U.S. 189 (1973).

44. Greene 1996, 33, citing *Milliken v. Bradley,* 418 U.S. 717 (1974).

45. At the time, of course, there was no Kiryas Joel school district. Presumably this was a copyediting error.

46. *Wieder,* 527 N.E.2d at 770, quoted in *Kiryas Joel* at 2485.

47. E.g., Greene 1996, 41, despite the fact that he emphasizes the overall Satmar community's "partial exit"; Eisgruber 1996, 94, despite

recognition of some equivocation in the record on whether or not Satmar is per se separatist; Lupu 1996, 117, despite his general lack of sympathy for Satmar "separatism."

48. Minow acknowledges that "[d]efining inclusion in public education for children with disabilities takes a different form . . . than inclusion for racial minorities" (1995, "Constitution," 18). She fails to recognize that the very existence of a debate among Kiryas Joel residents about how best to provide special education represents a massive step toward inclusion.

49. Minow points out that "[a]dvocates for disability rights might criticize the Village of Kiryas Joel for failing to provide inclusion or appropriate education for their disabled children within their own private, religious schools" (ibid., 19). Perhaps the majority of parents in the village would prefer to take government money and use it for special education within the yeshivas, thus promoting "inclusion" and "mainstreaming" of handicapped children within their home community. This the village cannot do. Again, what the Kiryas Joel dissenters object to are the constraints placed on the education of handicapped Hasidic children who benefit from state funding.

50. *Kiryas Joel* at 2495 (Stevens, J., concurring). Minow notes that the Stevens concurrence in *Kiryas Joel* is "consistent with Justice Stevens' view expressed in *Wallace v. Jaffree,* 472 U.S. 38, 50–55 (1985), that protection of individuals'—here, the schoolchildren's— freedom of conscience is the central focus of all the clauses of the First Amendment" (1995, "Constitution," 15).

51. *Kiryas Joel* at 2495 (Stevens, J., concurring).

52. It is certainly possible to mount a forceful argument for the Protestant model of toleration and freedom of religion as freedom of conscience but without separation of groups. Yet if "the children of both Kiryas Joel and Monroe-Woodbury will be worse off if they grow up to fear or despise their fellow citizens on the other side of the town line" (Eisgruber 1996, 101), does this mean that any form of parochial schooling is ultimately violative of children's rights and well-being? Against this it has been suggested that where "secular humanism" as a public school ideology "results in the establishment of a 'religion' . . . It might even lead to the radical conclusion that public education is unconstitutional per se" (Stolzenberg 1993, 589). The plausibility of claiming that either public education or

parochial education is illegitimate under the general principle of "freedom of religion" shows the near impossibility of reconciling the individual's "freedom to choose and change religion" with parental "freedom to transmit and implant religion in children" (Galanter 1966, 227–28).

Bibliography

Ackerman, B. 1980. *Social Justice in the Liberal State.* New Haven: Yale University Press.

Acklin, S. E. 1995. "Board of Education of Kiryas Joel School District v. Grumet: Another Snub for Lemon Draws It Nearer to Its Possible Demise." *Loyola Law Review* 41: 43–60.

Appiah, K. A. 1997. "Cosmopolitan Patriots." *Critical Inquiry* 23: 617–39.

Atran, S. 1989. "The Surrogate Colonization of Palestine, 1917–1939." *American Ethnologist* 16: 719–44.

Bakhtin, M. 1984. *Rabelais and His World.* Trans. H. Iswolsky. Bloomington: Indiana University Press.

Balibar, E. 1990. "Paradoxes of Universality." In *Anatomy of Racism,* ed. D. T. Goldberg, 283–94. Minneapolis: University of Minnesota Press.

Bartelson, J. 1995. *A Genealogy of Sovereignty.* Cambridge: Cambridge University Press.

Barton, C., and D. Boyarin. 2000. "Killing the Kids: Masada in Its Roman and Its Jewish Intertext." Paper presented at International Congress of Historical Sciences, Oslo.

Barton, C. A. 1993. *The Sorrows of the Ancient Romans: The Gladiator and the Monster.* Princeton: Princeton University Press.

———. 1994. "All Things Beseem the Victor: Paradoxes of Masculinity in Early Imperial Rome." In *Gender Rhetorics: Postures of Dominance and Submission in History,* ed. R. Trexler, 83–92. Albany: SUNY Press.

———. 1994. "Savage Miracles: The Redemption of Lost Honor in Roman Society and the Sacrament of the Gladiator and the Martyr." *Representations* 45 (winter): 41–71.

———. 1998. "The 'Moment of Truth' in Ancient Rome: Honor and Embodiment in a Contest Culture." *Stanford Humanities Review*: 16–30.

Bentham, J. 1975. *Principles of the Civil Code.*

Ben-Yehuda, N. 1995. *The Masada Myth: Collective Memory and Mythmaking in Israel.* Madison: University of Wisconsin Press.

Berg, T. C. 1995. "Slouching towards Secularism: A Comment on Kiryas Joel School District v. Grumet." *Emory Law Journal* 44: 433–99.

Berkowitz, M. 1996. *Western Jewry and the Zionist Project, 1914–1933.* Cambridge: Cambridge University Press.

Bernheimer, C. 1992. "Penile References in Phallic Theory." *Differences* 4, no. 1 (spring): 116–32.

Bersani, L. 1995. "Foucault, Freud, Fantasy, and Power." *GLQ* 2, no. 1–2 (special issue Pink Freud, ed. Diana Fuss): 11–33.

Bettelheim, B. 1954. *Symbolic Wounds: Puberty Rites and the Envious Male.* Glencoe, Ill.: Free Press.

Bhabha, H. K. 1983. "The Other Question: The Stereotype and Colonial Discourse." *Screen* 24, no. 6 (November–December).

———. 1994. *The Location of Culture.* London: Routledge.

Biale, D. 1986. *Power and Powerlessness in Jewish History.* New York: Schocken Books.

Biersteker, T. J., and C. Weber. 1996. Introduction to *State Sovereignty as Social Construct,* ed. T. J. Biersteker and C. Weber, 1–21. Cambridge Studies in Social Relations. Cambridge: Cambridge University Press.

Blacksher, J. U. 1995–96. "Majority Black Districts, Kiryas Joel, and Other Challenges to American Nationalism." *Cumberland Law Review* 26: 407–57.

Bowersock, G. W. 1995. *Martyrdom and Rome.* The Wiles Lectures Given at the Queen's University of Belfast. Cambridge: Cambridge University Press.

Boyarin, D. 1993. *Carnal Israel: Reading Sex in Talmudic Culture.*
New Historicism: Studies in Cultural Poetics, vol. 25. Berkeley
and Los Angeles: University of California Press.

———. 1994. *A Radical Jew: Paul and the Politics of Identity.*
Contraversions: Critical Studies in Jewish Literature, Culture,
and Society. Berkeley and Los Angeles: University of California
Press.

———. 1994. "Jewish Masochism: Couvade, Castration, and
Rabbis in Pain." *American Imago* 51, no. 1 (spring): 3–36.

———. 1997. *Unheroic Conduct: The Rise of Heterosexuality
and the Invention of the Jewish Man.* Contraversions: Critical
Studies in Jewish Literature, Culture, and Society. Berkeley
and Los Angeles: University of California Press.

———. 1999. *Dying for God: Martyrdom and the Making of Christianity and Judaism.* Lancaster/Yarnton Lectures in Judaism
and Other Religions for 1998. Stanford, Calif.: Stanford University Press.

———. 2000. "The Colonial Drag: Zionism, Gender, and Colonial
Mimicry." In *The Pre-occupation of Postcolonial Studies,* ed.
K. Seshadri-Crooks and F. Afzal-Kahn. Durham, N.C.: Duke
University Press.

Boyarin, J. 1992. *Storm from Paradise: The Politics of Jewish
Memory.* Minneapolis: University of Minnesota Press.

———. 1994. "Space, Time, and the Politics of Memory." In *Remapping Memory: The Politics of Timespace,* ed. J. Boyarin,
1–38. Minneapolis: University of Minnesota Press.

———. 1996. *Thinking in Jewish.* Chicago: University of Chicago
Press.

Breines, P. 1990. *Tough Jews: Political Fantasies and the Moral
Dilemma of American Jewry.* New York: Basic Books.

Briggs, S. 1985. "Images of Women and Jews in Nineteenth-
and Twentieth-Century German Theology." In *Immaculate
and Powerful: The Female in Sacred Image and Reality,* ed.
C. Atkinson, C. H. Buchanan, and M. Miles, 226–59. Boston:
Beacon Press.

Brooten, B. J. 1996. *Love between Women: Early Christian Responses
to Female Homoeroticism.* Chicago: University of Chicago
Press.

Brownstein, A. E. 1990. "Harmonizing the Heavenly and Earthly

Spheres: The Fragmentation and Synthesis of Religion, Equality, and Speech in the Constitution." *Ohio State Law Journal* 51: 89–174.

Burrus, V. 1994. "Fecund Fathers: Heresy, the Grotesque, and Male Generativity in Gregory of Nyssa's *Contra Eunomium.*" Unpublished paper, Madison, N.J.

———. 1995. *The Making of a Heretic: Gender, Authority, and the Priscillianist Controversy.* Transformations of the Ancient World. Berkeley and Los Angeles: University of California Press.

———. 1995. "Reading Agnes: 'The Rhetoric of Gender in Ambrose and Prudentius.'" *Journal of Early Christian Studies* 3, no. 1 (spring): 25–46.

Caldwell, S. L. 1987. "Begotten Not Made: Male Metaphors of Procreative Power." Master's thesis, University of California, Berkeley.

Cantor, A. 1995. *Jewish Women/Jewish Men: The Legacy of Patriarchy in Jewish Life.* San Francisco: HarperSanFrancisco.

Chambers, R. 1991. *Room for Maneuver: Reading (the) Oppositional (in) Narrative.* Chicago: University of Chicago Press.

Chandar, A. 2001. "Diaspora Bonds." *New York University Law Review* 76: 1005–99.

Chaterjee, P. 1990. "A Response to Taylor's 'Modes of Civil Society.'" *Public Culture* 3, no. 1: 119–34.

Churchill, W. 1996. "Like Sand in the Wind: The Making of an American Indian Diaspora in the United States." In *Geography and Identity: Living and Exploring Geopolitics of Identity,* ed. D. Crow, 246–79. Washington, D.C.: Maisonneuve.

Clastres, P. 1987. *Society against the State: Essays in Political Anthropology.* Trans. R. Hurley. New York: Zone Books.

Clifford, J. 1994. "Diasporas." *Cultural Anthropology* 9 (August): 302–38.

Cohen, R. 1996. *Global Diasporas: An Introduction.* Seattle: University of Washington Press.

Connolly, W. 1995. *The Ethics of Pluralization.* Minneapolis: University of Minnesota Press.

Cover, R. 1983. "The Supreme Court 1982 Term: Foreword: Nomos and Narrative." *Harvard Law Journal* 97:4–68.

Craft, C. 1995. *Another Kind of Love: Male Homosexual Desire in*

English Discourse, 1850–1920. New Historicism: Studies in Cultural Poetics, vol. 30. Berkeley and Los Angeles: University of California Press.

Daniel, J. L. 1979. "Anti-Semitism in the Hellenistic-Roman Period." *Journal of Biblical Literature* 98, no. 1: 45–65.

Davis, L. 1994. "Virgins in Brothels: A Different Feminist Reading of Beruriah." Paper presented at Graduate Theological Union, Berkeley, California.

Deleuze, G., and F. Guattari. 1986. *Kafka: Toward a Minor Literature.* Minneapolis: University of Minnesota Press.

———. 1987. *A Thousand Plateaus: Capitalism and Schizophrenia.* Minneapolis: University of Minnesota Press.

Dellamora, R. 1990. *Masculine Desire: The Sexual Politics of Victorian Aestheticism.* Chapel Hill: University of North Carolina Press.

Derrida, J. 1992. *The Other Heading: Reflections on Today's Europe.* Bloomington: University of Indiana Press.

Dijkstra, B. 1986. *Idols of Perversity: Fantasies of Feminine Evil in Fin-de-Siècle Culture.* New York: Oxford University Press.

Douglas, M. 1980. *Purity and Danger: An Analysis of Concepts of Pollution and Taboo.* Binghamton, N.Y.: Vail-Ballou Press.

Dubnow, S. 1931. "Diaspora." In *Encyclopaedia of the Social Sciences,* 126–30. New York: Macmillan.

Edelman, L. 1990. "Redeeming the Phallus: Wallace Stevens, Frank Lentricchia, and the Politics of (Hetero)Sexuality." In *Engendering Men,* ed. J. A. Boone and M. Cadden, 36–52. New York: Routledge.

Edwards, C. 1993. *The Politics of Immorality in Ancient Rome.* Cambridge: Cambridge University Press.

Eilberg-Schwartz, H. 1994. *God's Phallus and Other Problems for Men and Monotheism.* Boston: Beacon Press.

Eisgruber, C. L. 1996. "The Constitutional Value of Assimilation." *Columbia Law Review* 96: 87–103.

Feldman, Y. S. 1994. "'And Rebecca Loved Jacob,' but Freud Did Not." In *Freud and Forbidden Knowledge,* ed. P. L. Rudnytsky and E. H. Spitz, 7–25. New York: New York University Press.

Flusser, D., ed. and annotator. 1981. *The Josippon [Josephus Gorionides].* In Hebrew. Bialik Institute.

Ford, R. T. 1994. "The Boundaries of Race: Political Geography in Legal Analysis." *Harvard Law Review* 107: 1841–921.

Fout, J. C. 1992. "Sexual Politics in Wilhelmine German: The Male Gender Crisis, Moral Purity, and Homophobia." *Journal of the History of Sexuality* 2, no. 3: 388–421.

Fränkel, J. 1971. "Biblical Verses Quoted in Tales of the Sages." *Scripta Hiersolymitana* 22: 80–87.

Funkenstein, A. 1995. "The Dialectics of Assimilation." *Jewish Social Studies: History, Culture, and Society* 1, no. 2 (winter): 1–14.

Galanter, M. 1966. "Religious Freedoms in the United States: A Turning Point?" *Wisconsin Law Review*: 217.

Gallop, J. 1982. *The Daughter's Seduction: Feminism and Psychoanalysis*. Ithaca, N.Y.: Cornell University Press.

———. 1988. "Phallus/Penis: Same Difference." In *Thinking through the Body*, 124–33. New York: Columbia University Press.

Ganguly, K. 1992. "Migrant Identities, Personal Memory, and the Construction of Selfhood." *Cultural Studies* 6 (January).

Ghosh, A. 1989. "The Diaspora in Indian Culture." *Public Culture* 2, no. 1: 73–78.

Gilroy, P. 1993. *The Black Atlantic: Modernity and Double Consciousness*. Cambridge: Harvard University Press.

Gleason, M. W. 1995. *Making Men: Sophists and Self-Presentation in Ancient Rome*. Princeton: Princeton University Press.

Goldberg, H. 1977. "Culture and Ethnicity in the Study of Israeli Society." *Ethnic Groups* 1: 163–86.

Goldsmith, S. 1993. *Unbuilding Jerusalem: Apocalypse and Romantic Representation*. Ithaca, N.Y.: Cornell University Press.

Goldstein, M. 1957. "German Jewry's Dilemma: The Study of a Provocative Essay." *Leo Baeck Institute Yearbook* 2: 236–54.

Gottfried, B. 1988. "What *Do* Men Want, Dr. Roth?" In *A Mensch among Men: Explorations in Jewish Masculinity*, ed. H. Brod, 37–52. Freedom, Calif.: Crossing Press.

Gravdal, K. 1991. *Ravishing Maidens: Writing Rape in Medieval French Literature and Law*. Philadelphia: University of Pennsylvania Press.

Greene, A. S. 1996. "*Kiryas Joel* and Two Mistakes about Equality." *Columbia Law Review* 96: 1–86.

Hale, C. 1994. "'Wan Tasbaya Dukiara': Contested Notions of

Land Rights in Miskitu History." In *Remapping Memory: The Politics of Timespace,* ed. J. Boyarin, 67–98. Minneapolis: University of Minnesota Press.

Hall, D. E. 1994. "Muscular Christianity: Reading and Writing the Male Social Body." In *Muscular Christianity: Embodying the Victorian Age,* ed. D. E. Hall, 3–13. Cambridge Studies in Nineteenth-Century Literature and Culture, vol. 2. Cambridge: Cambridge University Press.

Hall, S. 1990. "Cultural Identity and Diaspora." In *Identity: Community, Culture, Difference,* ed. J. Rutherford, 222–37. London: Lawrence & Wishart.

Hartog, F. 1988. *The Mirror of Herodotus: The Representation of the Other in the Writing of History.* Trans. J. Lloyd. New Historicism. Berkeley and Los Angeles: University of California Press.

Harvey, D. 1989. *The Condition of Postmodernity: An Enquiry into the Origins of Cultural Change.* Oxford, England: Blackwell.

Hasan-Rokem, G. 2000. *The Web of Life: Folklore and Midrash in Rabbinic Literature.* Trans. B. Stein. Contraversions: Jews and Other Differences. Stanford, Calif.: Stanford University Press.

Hay, D. 1957. *Europe: The Emergence of an Idea.* Edinburgh: Edinburgh University Press.

Hempen, L. M. 1995. "Note: Board of Education of Kiryas Joel School District v. Grumet: Accomodationists Strike a Blow to the Wall of Separation." *St. Louis University Law Journal* 39: 1389–428.

Hoberman, J. M. 1995. "Otto Weininger and the Critique of Jewish Masculinity." In *Jews and Gender: Responses to Otto Weininger,* ed. N. A. Harrowitz and B. Hyams, 141–53. Philadelphia: Temple University Press.

Ilan, T. 1995. *Jewish Women in Greco-Roman Palestine.* Texte und Studien zum Antiken Judentum. Tübingen: J. C. B. Mohr (Paul Siebeck).

———. 1995. "Matrona and Rabbi Jose: An Alternative Interpretation." *Journal for the Study of Judaism in the Persian, Hellenistic, and Roman Periods* 25, no. 1: 18–51.

Jacobs, L. G. 1995. "Adding Complexity to Confusion and Seeing the Light: Feminist Legal Insights and the Jurisprudence of the Religion Clauses." *Yale Journal of Law and Feminism* 7: 137–72.

Jung, C. G. 1970. "The State of Psychotherapy Today." In *The Collected Works,* vol. 10, *Civilization in Transition,* trans. R. F. C. Hull. Bolingen Series, no. 20. Princeton, N.J.: Princeton University Press.

Kapferer, B. 1988. *Legends of People, Myths of State: Violence, Intolerance, and Political Culture in Sri Lanka and Australia.* Washington, D.C.: Smithsonian Institution Press.

Karst, K. L. 1986. "Paths to Belonging: The Constitution and Cultural Identity." *North Carolina Law Review* 64: 303–77.

Kirshenblatt-Gimblett, B. 1994. "Spaces of Dispersal." *Cultural Anthropology* 9, no. 3: 399–404.

Kristeva, J. 1986. "Word, Dialogue, and the Novel." In *The Kristeva Reader,* ed. T. Moi, 34–61. Oxford: Blackwell.

Kronfeld, C. 1996. *On the Margins of Modernism Decentering Literary Dynamics.* Contraversions: Critical Studies in Jewish Literature, Culture, and Society. Berkeley and Los Angeles: University of California Press.

Kuhns, J. 1995. *"Board of Education of Kiryas Joel Village School District v. Grumet*: The Supreme Court Shall Make No Law Defining an Establishment of Religion." *Pepperdine Law Review* 22: 1599–674.

Lakoff, G., and M. Johnson. 1980. *Metaphors We Live By.* Chicago: University of Chicago Press.

Lane, F. M. 1986. "The Genital Envy Complex: A Case of a Man with a Fantasied Vulva." In *The Psychology of Men: New Psychoanalytic Perspectives,* ed. G. I. Fogel, F. M. Lane, and R. S. Liebert, 131–51. New York: Basic Books.

Lavie, S., and T. Swedenburg. 1996. "Introduction: Displacement, Diaspora, and Geographies of Identity." In *Displacement, Diaspora, and Geographies of Identity,* ed. S. Lavie and T. Swedenburg, 1–25. Durham, N.C.: Duke University Press.

Lefkowitz, L. 1988. "Coats and Tales: Joseph Stories and Myths of Jewish Masculinity." In *A Mensch among Men: Explorations in Jewish Masculinity,* ed. H. Brod, 19–29. Freedom, Calif.: Crossing Press.

Legendre, P. 1985. *L'Inestimable objet de la transmission: Étude sur le principe généalogique en Occident.* Paris: Fayard.

Le Rider, J. 1995. "The 'Otto Weininger Case' Revisited." In *Jews and Gender: Responses to Otto Weininger,* ed. N. A. Harrowitz and B. Hyams, 21–33. Philadelphia: Temple University Press.

Levine, A.-J. 1992. "Diaspora as Metaphor: Bodies and Boundaries in the Book of Tobit." In *Diaspora Jews and Judaism: Essays in Honor of, and in Dialogue with, A. Thomas Kraabel,* ed. J. A. Overman and R. S. MacLennan, 105–18. South Florida Studies in the History of Judaism. Atlanta: Scholars Press.

Levinson, S. 1988. *Constitutional Faith.* Princeton, N.J.: Princeton University Press.

Levy, L. W. 1994. *The Establishment Clause: Religion and the First Amendment.* Chapel Hill: University of North Carolina Press.

Lieberman, S. 1939–1944. "The Martyrs of Caesarea." *Annuaire de l'institut de philologie et d'histoire orientales et slaves* 7: 395–446.

Lipkin, R. J. 1995. "Liberalism and the Possibility of Multi-Cultural Constitutionalism: The Distinction between Deliberative and Dedicated Cultures." *University of Richmond Law Review* 29: 1263–325.

Loraux, N. 1995. *The Experiences of Tiresias: The Feminine and the Greek Man.* Princeton, N.J.: Princeton University Press.

Lupu, I. C. 1987. "Free Exercise Exemption and Religious Institutions: The Case of Employment Discrimination." *Boston University Law Review* 67: 391–442.

———. 1996. "Uncovering the Village of Kiryas Joel." *Columbia Law Review* 96: 104–20.

Luxon, T. J. 1995. Letter to the author.

Malkki, L. 1994. "Citizens of Humanity: Internationalism and the Imagined Community of Nations." *Diaspora* 3, no. 1: 41–68.

Martin, D. B. 1990. *Slavery as Salvation: The Metaphor of Slavery in Pauline Christianity.* New Haven: Yale University Press.

Mattelart, A. 1994. *Mapping World Communication: War, Progress, Culture.* Trans. S. Emanuel and J. A. Cohen. Minneapolis: University of Minnesota Press.

McLean, I. 1992–93. "'The Circumference Is Everywhere and the Centre Nowhere': Modernity and the Diasporic Discovery of Columbus as Told by Tzvetan Todorov." *Third Text* 24: 5–10.

Miller, N. K. 1990. "The Text's Heroine: A Feminist Critic and Her Fictions." In *Conflicts in Feminism,* ed. M. Hirsch and E. F. Keller, 112–20. New York: Routledge.

Miller, P. 1956. *Errand into the Wilderness.* Cambridge: Harvard University Press, Belknap Press.

Minow, M. 1995. "The Constitution and the Subgroup Question." *Indiana Law Journal* 71: 1–25.

———. 1995. "Rights and Cultural Difference." In *Identities, Politics, and Rights,* 347–65. Ann Arbor: University of Michigan Press.

Mintz, A. 1984. *Hurban: Responses to Catastrophe in Hebrew Literature.* New York: Columbia University Press.

Mintz, J. 1992. *Hasidic People: A Place in the New World.* Cambridge: Harvard University Press.

Mishra, V. 1994. [Untitled]. *Center for Cultural Studies Newsletter.* University of California, Santa Cruz.

———. 1996. "The Diasporic Imaginary: Theorizing the Indian Diaspora." *Textual Practice* 10: 421–47.

Modleski, T. 1991. *Feminism without Women: Culture and Criticism in a "Postfeminist" Age.* New York: Routledge.

Mosse, G. L. 1985. *Nationalism and Sexuality: Middle-Class Morality and Sexual Norms in Modern Europe.* Madison: University of Wisconsin Press.

Murphy, A. B. 1996. "The Sovereign State System as Political-Territorial Ideal: Historical and Contemporary Considerations." In *State Sovereignty as Social Construct,* 81–120. Cambridge: Cambridge University Press.

Nancy, J.-L. 1991. *The Inoperative Community.* Minneapolis: University of Minnesota Press.

Nandy, A. 1990. "Dialogue and the Diaspora." *Third Text* 11.

Nerlich, M. 1987. *Ideology of Adventure: Studies in Modern Consciousness, 1100–1750,* vol. 2. Trans. R. Crowley. Theory and History of Literature, vol. 43. Minneapolis: University of Minnesota Press.

Neuchterlein, J. E. 1990. "The Free Exercise Boundaries of Permissible Accommodation under the Establishment Clause." *Yale Law Journal* 99: 1127–46.

Neusner, J. 1970. *A Life of Yohanan ben Zakkai.* Leiden: E. J. Brill.

———. 1981. *Judaism: The Evidence of the Mishna.* Chicago: University of Chicago Press.

Nordau, M. 1980. "Muskeljudentum." In *The Jew in the Modern*

World: A Documentary History, ed. P. R. Mendes-Flohr and
J. Reinharz, 434–35. New York: Oxford University Press.

Olivo, C. L. 1993. "Note: Grumet vs. Board of Education of the
Kiryas Joel Village School District—When Neutrality Masks
Hostility—The Exclusion of Religious Communities from an
Entitlement to Public Schools." *Notre Dame Law Review* 68:
775–817.

Ong, A. 1998. "Flexible Citizenship among Chinese Cosmopolitans."
In *Cosmopolitics: Thinking and Feeling beyond the Nation*, ed.
Pheng Cheah and B. Robbins. Minneapolis: University of
Minnesota Press.

Pateman, C. 1988. *The Sexual Contract*. Stanford, Calif.: Stanford
University Press.

Pearce, R. H. 1988. *Savagism and Civilization: A Study of the Indian
and the American Mind*. Berkeley and Los Angeles: University
of California Press.

Perkins, J. 1995. *The Suffering Self: Pain and Narrative Representation in the Early Christian Era*. London: Routledge.

Pildes, R. H., and R. G. Niemi. 1993. "Expressive Harms, 'Bizarre
Districts,' and Voting Rights: Evaluating Election-District
Appearances after Shaw v. Reno." *Michigan Law Review* 92:
483–587.

Portugali, Y. 1988. "Nationalism, Social Theory, and the Israeli/
Palestinian Case." In *Nationalism, Self-Determination, and
Political Geography*, ed. R. Johnston, D. Knight, and E. Kofman,
151–65. London: Croon Helm.

Ramas, M. 1980. "Freud's Dora, Dora's Hysteria: The Negation of
a Woman's Rebellion." *Feminist Studies* 6, no. 3 (fall): 472–510.

Rawls, J. 1971. *A Theory of Justice*. Cambridge: Harvard University
Press, Belknap Press.

Reisman, M. 1993. "Autonomy, Interdependence, and Responsibility."
Yale Law Journal 103: 401–17.

Reynolds, K., and N. Humble. 1993. *Victorian Heroines: Representations of Femininity in Nineteenth-Century Literature and
Art*. New York: New York University Press.

Richlin, A. 1992. *The Garden of Priapus: Sexuality and Aggression
in Roman Humor*. 2d ed. New York: Oxford University Press.

Rosenfeld, A., trans. and ed. 1978. *The Authorised Selichot for
the Whole Year according to the Rite in Use among Hebrew*

Congregations in the Commonwealth and in Central Europe.
New York: Judaica Press.

Rubin, I. 1972. *Satmar: An Island in the City.* Chicago: Quadrangle
Books.

Saldarini, A. 1975. "Johanan ben Zakkai's Escape from Jerusalem:
Origin and Development of a Rabbinic Story." *Journal for
the Study of Judaism in the Persian, Hellenistic, and Roman
Periods* 6: 189–220.

Scheid, J., and J. Svenbro. 1996. *The Craft of Zeus: Myths of
Weaving and Fabric.* Revealing Antiquity, vol. 9. Cambridge:
Harvard University Press.

Schochet, G. 1975. *Patriarchalism in Political Thought: The
Authoritarian Family and Political Speculation and Attitudes
Especially in Seventeenth-Century England.* Oxford: Basil
Blackwell.

Schütz, A. 1995. "Sons of Writ, Sons of Wrath: Pierre Legendre's
Critique of Rational Law-Giving." *Cardozo Law Journal* 16:
979–1022.

Schweitzer, C. B. 1995. "Note: Board of Education of Kiryas Joel
School District v. Grumet, 114 S. Ct. 2481 (1994)." *Duquesne
Law Review* 33: 1007–31.

Scott, J. C. 1990. *Domination and the Arts of Resistance: Hidden
Transcripts.* New Haven: Yale University Press.

Seal, W. O., Jr. 1995. "'Benevolent Neutrality' toward Religion: Still
an Elusive Ideal after *Board of Education of Kiryas Joel v.
Grumet.*" *North Carolina Law Review* 73: 1641–76.

Segal, D. A. 1994. "Living Ancestors: Nationalism and the Past in
Post-colonial Trinidad and Tobago." In *Remapping Memory:
The Politics of Timespace,* 221–40. Minneapolis: University
of Minnesota Press.

Shain, Y. 1994. "Marketing the Democratic Creed Abroad: US
Diaspora Politics in the Era of Multiculturalism." *Diaspora* 3,
no. 1: 85–111.

Siegel, C. 1995. *Male Masochism: Modern Revisions of the Story of
Love.* Bloomington: Indiana University Press.

Silverman, K. 1992. "The Lacanian Phallus." *Differences* 4, no. 1
(spring): 84–115.

———. 1992. *Male Subjectivity at the Margins.* New York:
Routledge.

Simon, E. 1956. "Jewish Adult Education in Nazi Germany as Spiritual Resistance." *Leo Baeck Institute Year Book* 1: 68–104.

Skinner, E. P. 1982. "The Dialectic between Diasporas and Homelands." In *Global Dimensions of the African Diaspora*, ed. J. E. Harris, 11–40. Washington, D.C.: Howard University Press.

Smith, S. 1995. *Foreordained Failure: The Quest for a Constitutional Principle of Religious Freedom*. New York: Oxford University Press.

Spiegel, S. 1967. *The Last Trial on the Legends and Lore of the Command to Abraham to Offer Isaac as a Sacrifice: The Akedah*. Trans. J. Goldin. New York: Pantheon.

Spivak, G. C. 1989. "Who Claims Alterity?" In *Remaking History*, ed. B. Kruger and P. Mariani, 269–92. Seattle: Bay Press.

———. 1990. "Constitutions and Culture Studies." *Yale Journal of Law and the Humanities* 2: 133–47.

Stock, B. 1990. *Listening for the Text: On the Uses of the Past*. Parallax: Re-visions of Culture and Society. Baltimore: Johns Hopkins University Press.

Stolzenberg, N. M. 1993. "'He Drew a Circle That Shut Me Out': Assimilation, Indoctrination, and the Paradox of a Liberal Education." *Harvard Law Review* 106: 581–667.

Stone, S. L. 1993. "In Pursuit of the Counter-Text: The Turn to the Jewish Legal Model in Contemporary Legal Theory." *Harvard Law Review* 106: 813–94.

Stratton, J. 2000. *Coming Out Jewish*. New York: Routledge.

Theodor, J., and H. Albeck, eds. 1965. *Genesis Rabbah*. Jerusalem: Wahrmann.

Thomas, S. B. 1994. "Beyond a Sour Lemon: A Look at *Grumet v. Board of Education of the Kiryas Joel Village School District*, 114 S. Ct. 2482 (1994)." *BYU Journal of Public Law* 8: 531–52.

Todorov, T. 1984. *The Conquest of America: The Question of the Other*. New York: Harper and Row.

Trumpener, K. 1992. "The Time of the Gypsies: A 'People without History' in the Narratives of the West." *Critical Inquiry* 18, no. 4: 843–84.

Vidal-Naquet, P. 1983. "Josephus Flavius and Masada." *Zemanim* 13: 67–75.

Walzer, M. 1983. *Spheres of Justice*. New York: Basic Books.

Weinreich, M. 1980. *The History of the Yiddish Language*. Trans.
S. Noble and J. Fishman. Chicago: University of Chicago Press.

Weyrauch, W. O., and M. A. Bell. 1993. "Autonomous Lawmaking:
The Case of the 'Gypsies.'" *Yale Law Journal* 103, no. 2: 323–99.

Wheeler, A. 1995. "Separatist Religious Groups and the Establishment
Clause: *Board of Education of Kiryas Joel School District v.
Grumet,* 114 S. Ct. 2482 (1994)." *Harvard Civil Rights: Civil
Liberties Law Review* 30: 223–46.

White, H. 1981. "The Value of Narrativity in the Representation
of Reality." In *On Narrativity,* ed. W. Mitchell, 1–23. Chicago:
University of Chicago Press.

Wiedemann, T. 1992. *Emperors and Gladiators*. New York:
Routledge.

Witte, J. R. 1996. "The Essential Rights and Liberties of Religion
in the American Constitutional Experiment." *Notre Dame
Law Review* 71: 371–445.

Yadin, Y. 1966. *Masada: Herod's Fortress and the Zealots' Last
Stand*. London: Weidenfeld & Nicolson.

Zeitlin, F. 1996. *Playing the Other: Gender and Society in Classical
Greek Literature*. Women in Culture and Society, 53–86.
Chicago: University of Chicago Press.

Zertal, I. 1994. "The Sacrificed and the Sanctified: The Construction
of a National Martyrology." *Zemanim* 12, no. 48 (spring):
26–45.

Zerubavel, Y. 1994. "The Death of Memory and the Memory of
Death: Masada and the Holocaust as Historical Metaphors."
Representations 45 (winter): 72–100.

———. 1995. *Recovered Roots: Collective Memory and the Making
of Israeli National Tradition*. Chicago: University of Chicago
Press.

Index

Martin, Dale B., 143–44 n. 57

Martyrdom: early Christian, 43; early Jewish, 37, 64–65; as manly (Roman view), 53, 54, 63, 140 n. 39; Zionist appropriation of, 52–53

Masada myth: the fall of Masada, 46, 47; historically questionable, 47–50, 136 n. 13; intertextual comparisons of, 51–53; in Josephus, 47, 49, 135 n. 1; omission from rabbinic Judaism, 47–48, 50, 135 n. 12; rabbinic version, 50–51

Masculinity. *See* Masculinity in Jewish culture; Phallic masculinity

Masculinity in Jewish culture, 40, 45–46, 78; disempowered maleness and, 43–44, 78; metaphors of feminine procreative power in, 78, 89, 90, 100, 101; nonphallic models of, 73–74, 77, 78–81, 89–90, 93, 99; self-femminization and, 100. *See also* Femminization; Penis

Matrona, 88, 144 n. 58

Mattelart, Armand, 5, 26

Meʿir, Rabbi, 71–72

Memory, Jewish, 47, 76

Mennonite religious communities, 112, 149 n. 16

Merneptah, 37

Mexican emigration to the U.S., 7

Midrash, 80

Migration, 27–28; as immigration, 9, 10

Miller, Nancy K., 43

Milliken v. Bradley, 122, 123

Minority group status, 105, 116; religious minorities and, 119–20

Minow, Martha, 105, 113–14, 116, 153 n. 29, 156 n. 48

Mintz, A., 11, 124

Mirroring, 84

Mishra, Vijay, 14–15

Misogyny, 58, 75

Modleski, Tanya, 85–86

Monroe-Woodbury School district, 107, 123–24

Montana Militia, 117

"Mosaic" approach to state constituencies, 9–10

Moses, 1–2, 3

Mother/son relationship, 80

Multiculturalism, 22, 24, 33. *See also* Pluralism

"Muscular Jews." *See* Neo-machismo in Jewish culture

Nahnu-ma (nothingness), 1–4

Naphtali tribe, 133–34 n. 3

Narrative models in jurisprudence, 112

Narratives, 112; judicial, 111–12; oppositional, 7

Nation-state: approaches to state constituencies, 9–10, 24; diasporic communities and, 9–10, 18–19, 23; homelands of diasporic communities, 15, 22, 29; "host" countries to diasporic communities, 8; legitimization crisis of, 10; nation-state system, 5–6, 9;

JONATHAN BOYARIN is a lawyer and an independent scholar of anthropology and Jewish cultural studies. He has carried out fieldwork in Paris, Jerusalem, and the Lower East Side of New York City, where he has lived for the past twenty years. He is author of *Polish Jews in Paris, Storm from Paradise: The Politics of Jewish Memory* (Minnesota, 1992), *Thinking in Jewish,* and *From a Ruined Garden* (with Jack Kugelmass); he is coeditor (with Daniel Boyarin) of *Jews and Other Differences: The New Jewish Cultural Studies* (Minnesota, 1997).

DANIEL BOYARIN is Taubman Professor of Talmudic Culture in the departments of Near Eastern studies and rhetoric at the University of California at Berkeley. His most recent books include *Unheroic Conduct: The Rise of Heterosexuality and the Invention of the Jewish Man* and *Dying for God: Martyrdom and the Making of Christianity and Judaism.* He is coeditor (with Jonathan Boyarin) of *Jews and Other Differences: The New Jewish Cultural Studies* (Minnesota, 1997).